THE FUTURE OF SELLING WITH THE
TRUSTED ADVISOR METHOD

SELLING IN THE NEW WORLD

HOW TO RE-THINK, RE-TOOL, RE-SKILL IN
THE NEW SALES WORLD

BRAD TONINI

The future of selling with the
Trusted Advisor Method

SELLING IN THE NEW WORLD

How to re-think, re-tool, re-skill in
the new sales world

BRAD TONINI

TRUSTED ADVISOR PRESS

1213/1 Queens Road, Melbourne, Australia
brad@bradtonini.com

ISBN: 978-0-6489112-5-8   PAPERBACK
ISBN: 978-0-6489112-6-5   HARDBACK

Cover and interior design *LRB Publishing Services*
contact@lindaruthbrooks.com
Nonfiction/sales education/
SELLING IN THE NEW WORLD is a sales instruction manual, designed to assist salespersons of all areas to gain valuable information on ways to optimise sales opportunities through presentation, high standard behaviour and becoming trusted advisors to their clients. Every attempt has been made to give appropriate acknowledgment for material, visual or written.

Time for Life

Make It Happen Now!

The New Rules of the Game

101 Ways to Keep the Sales Focus

Sales 101

7 Keys to Presenting Ideas That Sell

The Great Theatre of the Sale

The New Sales Leader – How to Transform the Sales Team!

To my dad Neville Tonini, the greatest salesman of them all.

Each day was a selling opportunity, delivered with great charisma and showmanship.

Contents

Introduction – Selling in the New World

At the end of the day, without the sale there is no business.

I made this point in a workshop and I think a salesperson at the seminar took the idea too far. He made a point of letting other people in the business know when he got back to the office that if he didn't perform, then no one would have a job.

I wouldn't recommend you do that if you intend to retain strong internal relationships in the workplace; however, I will state my bias that sales is a critical function in any company.

The future of selling is in relationships and you could say it always has been. But recently, something shifted, a new paradigm in how we connect with people and relate to their plight. We were moved by a pandemic which changed everyone's mindsets and made us take a more holistic view of selling.

Suddenly we were in a position where we couldn't go out and see our customers and had to do all the contact work on the email and via virtual means like Zoom or Google Meet. I think these times will create some new thinking about the new way business is done.

We learned that buyers are people who want to know you care and that you are going to hold their interests at heart. This might sound fanciful, but I think the salespeople who make transparency and genuineness a priority will be at a distinct advantage in the new market.

Flexibility in your thinking will be a sought-after trait in the new selling world by sales managers and business owners. As economies recover, we have to be patient, to stay the course.

I guess as we go on this journey together, I should tell you a little about me to give you context as to why this book, why now, and who this guy is.

I've grown up with selling. It's in my DNA. From a young age I witnessed feature/benefit selling, value selling, consultative selling, and many other trends. My dad, Neville Tonini, taught me about selling from a very young age and was entrepreneurial and very much a salesman. I'd get a motivational talk every day across the breakfast table in between "pass the vegemite and jam."

I was lucky enough to go out on my first appointments with him when I entered the business world. I learned so many lessons, amongst the best ones were the power of getting excited about your idea, to do the work to create something of real value, and to believe in yourself through and through.

He was an important mentor.

My first business was a tennis coaching business for local would-be John McEnroes. You can't sell tennis lessons to people who aren't suited to tennis; they are going to want their money back the next week and this paid the petrol and living expenses each week.

It gave me some extra cash to pay the bills while I fumbled my way through university with my marketing degree. After nine years attending part time at night and three deferments due to wanting to get out there and earn a crust, I made it.

In 2008, I sold my last business in executive diaries and promotional products in a very commoditised industry. It's funny as so many of the salespeople I teach and coach say to me, "You don't understand how commoditised our industry is." Try selling a range of diaries in the Australian and New Zealand markets; there are only so many ways you can print and bind a diary to make it revolutionary!

I guess it was in the sale of the business where I learned the power of systems, structures, and building a turnkey business or "E-Mything the business." Thanks, Mr. Gerber.

After 35 years around sales, some old things become new again. That's true. However, I would call these tried and proven ways to sell, as well as those things we need to make a priority.

Now having coached thousands of salespeople here and overseas in the Trusted Advisor Selling Method and sales managers on how to become great sales leaders, I am convinced that no one has all the answers, but together a great deal can be achieved when you get great sales minds around a table.

The new world is one where we need to explore new ways of going to market, to keep yourself and your message relevant to more sophisticated and information-rich buyers.

My premise is that it is the perfect time for us to re-tool and re-set our selling efforts, and I will talk more about that in the next few chapters. Using the opportunity to get better and be more relevant is a good use of your time.

Collaboration is the way we can acquire clients in the new world with a low cost of acquisition and much shorter selling cycles. It's about being so much more strategic with your time.

We learned all about the power of the virtual world in our selling through the pandemic and I think it has a really important role to play moving forward. Innovative salespeople get this.

I call it blended account servicing, where you can still do the face-to-face account service calls but also introduce another level of servicing on Zoom or a similar platform. Blended account servicing is a clever way to service the long tail in your selling business.

The power of connecting and nurturing is an increasingly important way of developing the new lead and then converting the business, but it takes patience.

Customer sales calls will continue to be like gold and we will need to "up the ante" in terms of what we deliver to the customer by creating experiences and not just a regular drop-by sales calls with no real agenda.

Autonomous sales teams are going to be more of the future of selling, the truth is that we have gotten used to the idea of having to work by ourselves, and business owners are continually going to question whether or not they need to make the investment in commercial premises.

Of course, that creates a need for better and better ways to monitor KPIs and to set the expectations for business owners and sales managers. The great thing though is that as a salesperson, you can set your own week, and as long as you are delivering results, you can run your business inside the business.

It's a new selling world out there and this book is directed at giving the tools to being successful in sales by playing by the new rules.

Welcome to the new world of selling.

Part 1

SELLING HAS CHANGED FOREVER

Why we need to re-tool and re-set our selling efforts

Chapter 1
The market wants relevance, are you ready?

Selling has gone through the biggest transformation I have seen in my 35 years in sales. In recent times, we have learned the true value of connecting and reaching out to others, and there will continue to be a shift in the way we sell, from selling to being of service to our clients first before we have earned the right to ask for their business.

For some who were industry hoppers, it's no longer all about just making quick sales and moving on, it's about making a difference in the lives of others. Pushy, insincere salespeople sell at their peril as buyers are looking for relationships, perhaps ones that even transcend the business partnership.

The 2020s and beyond will be a much more challenging selling environment with some risk averse buyers requiring salespeople to make the business case as to why they should buy and part ways with the funds.

There will also be a reluctance to change from the incumbent as that would take more work for an under-resourced procurement department. However, don't take your clients for granted as they will be also looking for savings, so make sure you are the lowest total cost solution. Notice I didn't say the cheapest, more about that later.

The premium placed on face-to-face meetings now by buyers since we have gotten used to working virtually means that you better have something to say of value! Virtual conversations with clients via Zoom and other means have shifted our thinking about how we engage our buyers, and buyers don't always need to be seen face-to-face anymore.

The road to relevance

Our biggest challenge as salespeople is to remain relevant to the market we serve. Apart from spending the money and demanding better value from those who provide goods and services to us, they want someone who gets them.

It's up to us more than ever to not just be a salesperson but to be an active friend, confidant, and partner in their business. I call it a Trusted Advisor, a vendor they can trust and are happy with which to work.

Relevance is about being current, to put yourself in the other person's shoes, and to be well positioned to be the right salesperson and right organisation for your buyer. Buyers are going to seek more and more the "right fit" relationship.

Relevance means tailoring your message, changing your offering, and making a sharp right turn on your language. Being flexible and nimble to change as we navigate the new arena.

I think it will be really important to continually ask ourselves these questions:

Do I still have a compelling proposition for the market or does it need to be re-sculptured?

Talking about your company history and how you offer up your competitive advantage to the market may be obsolete unless you can tie your message to what it can do for the customer or prospective client.

By not talking about your values, what you stand for, and how you deliver on the promise with an iron clad guarantee, does your message then lack real bite in this relevance marketplace?

How about the unique packages I offer? Do I need to re-bundle or re-model my offering?

If you have not developed new solutions to market by reverse engineering back from what you are hearing from the customer and the prospect, you may be missing out on opportunities. The market has shifted.

Are there new price points I need to consider to have the customer try before they really buy?

Not discounting, just a new layer of price points that allow the buyer to sample or place that trial order, and then the onus is back on us to "peddle like crazy," as my dad put it, to ascend the buyer into a fully-fledged partner for the long term.

Does it make sense to develop a new alliance so my offering becomes more comprehensive and thus making the life of the customer even easier?

If it makes the buyer's life easier because they can go to one person or one organisation rather than deal with multiple vendors, can you offer a simple way to buy?

Do I need to re-brand as a company, or how about me as a personal brand? Do I need to refresh the way I market?

Do the tools of the trade like website, collateral, positioning statement all need to be looked at to reflect how you help your customers and add value to their business?

Sales managers are also not exempt in the new relevant world. In fact, their role is even more important as a sales leader; how about their relevance to the sales team?

As the leader, is your messaging, communication, and coaching relevant to the team? And how do you make sure that the whole team is on the same page with how you interact with your customers?

As new salespeople get recruited into sales teams as we move forward, do you have a relevant induction program so you can build competitive advantage in the market?

Relevance is the key word in selling now. Relevance in how you connect, how you attract new business, how you convert the business, and how you expand the business.

Take prospecting, for example. Pure activity for activity's sake is just plain stupid in this market. Be more strategic, think what actions will really net you the results.

Learn to work your base harder, to connect with people who know you and appreciate your value, and enlist their help in growing your business.

If you are of the old school of "close everything" and to convince the buyer to buy, you will be playing by rules that no longer always apply. Working harder, harder, and harder to get a lesser return.

Think about activity differently: reaching out and making more calls than ever, not in terms of the confirmed sale perhaps but to get a feel for the market and your customer and prospect base by connecting and nurturing.

To assume will trip up the novice salesperson as they navigate this new reality.

Understanding people's situations is key; you may be surprised that some of your customers are actually thriving in this environment.

Right place, right product at the right time.

Trust unlocks the door to being relevant in this market; trust that you will do what you say, trust that you will follow through, trust that you will lead with transparency and integrity.

Developing the right language of the sale, to speak with

clarity, and to be proactive by thinking multiple steps ahead are all important skills in the new relevance market.

Selling in the New World Imperative:

Business has had a re-set. Do your selling efforts reflect that or are you still selling the same old way and realising that it's just not getting the results you deserve?

Chapter 2

Inside the new buyer's mind: 10 things they do and don't want

If I ask the question in my workshops, "What's changed about selling in the last 15-20 years in dealing with your buyers?" I always get a number of hands go up. Perhaps it's an opportunity as a salesperson to share an old war story about how much harder it is now compared to the good ole days?

I ask the question because I am trying to shift the selling minds in the room from thinking of "how to sell to someone" to understanding more about "how buyers buy."

The salesperson in the future who can spend as much time as possible being a student of buyer behaviour, buyer drivers, and motivations will be a desired commodity for sales teams.

It really isn't about us. It's all about them. In fact, it's always been about them! When I talk about selling in this new world, smart salespeople need to understand what is at the forefront of the buyer's mind.

Here are **10 distinctions** that are critical:

1. Buyers in the new selling world don't want more information.

"Infobesity" is the word currently used to describe the glut of information available at everybody's fingertips. Old-style salespeople get caught in a time warp and press on with "features and benefits selling" that worked in the distant past. I recall those days too. We used to take catalogues out to prospects and talk their heads off, but not anymore.

Buyers are more educated than ever before. Technology has placed information at everybody's fingertips. Features and benefits selling is no longer the only game in town.

> *The Trusted Advisor's focus in the new world:*
> *Selling is not all about features and benefits;*
> *this stuff can be downloaded. It's all about*
> *storytelling, visual imagery, and going on a*
> *journey with thought-provoking questions.*
> *Make yourself memorable.*

2. The new buyer is busier than ever in this world.

People trust professionals.

Demonstrate your professionalism by not wasting the buyer's time and by responding quickly to enquiries.

Your buyer's time is the most valuable asset they've got. They don't need to meet you unless there's something to discuss. Don't restate what they already know. Tell them something they can't find on the internet.

With companies being under resourced for a while in this new world, buyers are going to be stretched everywhere and helping to cover the bases. The secret is to make it easy for them.

Not being responsive is an absolute no-no in sales. It's an approach you'd like to see in your competitor! Speed things up a little. If you can't keep up with sales now, you'll be left behind.

3. Buyers can't determine the tiny differences between most competing products.

Product differences are decreasing between competing brands. Examples: generic peanuts vs. branded peanuts, this fridge vs. that fridge, this ream of A4 paper vs. that ream.

The difference between anything from soap to same-class vehicles is very little.

Ask yourself, what is it they want?

Answer: They want outcomes, and that's never changed.

It's never been easier to start a business from a logistics point of view. All you need do is create a website, a Facebook page, and a LinkedIn profile and you're in up and running for a few thousand bucks.

The disadvantage is there are innumerable competitors because they can do the same.

> *The Trusted Advisor's focus in the new world:*
> *Offer a total solution to their problem. You've*
> *got the experience and expertise. You've seen*
> *it work to your previous buyers' satisfaction.*
> *Show your new enquirers how that was*
> *achieved. Advise them.*

4. The new buyer wants to commoditise you.

Some people say there are only two places to be in the market: the premium end or the bottom end.

They don't want to be lost in the murky middle. That's a terrible place to be.

It's "me too" and "no apparent differentiation."

Premium products keep selling in the marketplace because of brand, perception of trust, the company's reputation, and a perception of value.

Good salespeople have a way of flagging the value when they have that conversation. A quality salesperson can always hold margin in the deal.

*The Trusted Advisor's focus in the new world:
Find a different way of presenting. Maybe
bundle your product in a different way. Make
it sound authoritative. Show that you can
make their life easier by purchasing top-of-
the-range products while also reminding them
that as a Trusted Advisor, your value has
never been more important.*

5. Buyers will continue trying to diminish the sales process.

Requests For Proposals (RFPs) have commoditised the buying process.

Buyers are saying, "I don't want to talk to a salesperson unless I have to. I'll send out a spreadsheet. S/he can fill it out for me, write a price on the bottom, and send it back."

That's a whole different selling game and it's happening more and more, especially with government and council purchasing.

What game do you want to play in the new world?

You could sit back and let it all happen or you could fight back. You also could resist the whole process by choosing not to quote.

You may spend hours putting together a quote, which may turn into a total time waster.

The Trusted Advisor's focus in the new world: If you come from the law of scarcity, you'll quote on everything. If you come from the law of abundance (i.e., believing there are more people out there who could use your services), you can afford to resist.

6. Our buyer expects you to be connected.

Not everybody wants to get into Instagram or Facebook, but social media has a professional function and that's here to stay. Ignore at your peril.

Its function is about building a business. But here's the trap that a lot of salespeople have fallen into. They believe that sitting at a desk and Facebooking is selling. It's not.

Some salespeople will explain their use of social media in the workplace with the words,

"I'm prospecting," or, "I sent out 30 invitations on Facebook."

They're kidding themselves. That's not selling, it's "connecting."

LinkedIn is my medium of choice; that's where your market in business-to-business is hiding out.

Connect without hooks, be of service, and show a genuine interest in others, then nurture the relationship.

7. The buyer is sick of "turn up and suck up" customer visits.

Back in the old days of selling, salespeople had a regular call cycle where they simply turned up with the brochures and samples and chatted while bringing the brochures out one-by-one.

That was their spiel.

Most answers that customers need can be given over the phone or by email, and they would much more prefer to deal that way rather than having the sales representative turn up and expect to be entertained while they are trying to run their business.

The buyer will always make time for the salesperson who they think has something of value to say.

Be the industry expert in the new selling world and someone they have time for, someone with real expertise.

*The Trusted Advisor's focus in the new world:
Have a real reason for being there, talk
succinctly, and captivate your customers by
telling them something they can't possibly
know or download from your webpage. Act on
a promise, deliver on your last conversation
and you will be welcomed into their business.*

8. Buyers want you to help them.

The old adage was that it costs six times as much to create a new customer as hanging on to an old one. I'm sure that getting a new customer versus selling to an existing one is more like 20 times now. Selling in the new world means that there is a higher cost of acquiring new customers than ever before. So you've got to hang onto them and be an expert in looking for organic growth than ever before.

It's up to us as Trusted Advisors to ensure we're making clients aware of where people are at, what their history is, and how many years they've been in the market they're in.

*The Trusted Advisor's focus in the new world:
The way to cut through and create new
customers is through a trusted source. Trust
is the new currency and it will create leverage
for opening up new referred doors.*

9. Rote learned sales techniques won't work on them!

Throw out all the manipulative sales techniques. Customers spot them a mile away. They read about them in magazines, see them exposed on news programs, get internet warnings, and are exposed to the sales books. If there's anything left, they've accessed that too.

Don't just flog them stuff. To create buyer engagement, work out <u>how</u> they buy, not <u>what</u> you're going to sell them. Question: "What drives this customer?"

> *The Trusted Advisor's focus in the new world:*
> *It's so important to have a conversation when*
> *you're selling, instead of shamelessly*
> *mouthing off sales patter that's been around*
> *for 30 years. If I hear another salesperson ask,*
> *"What keeps you awake at night?" I think I*
> *will lose it!*

10. Your buyer doesn't want to be HARD SOLD to in this new world.

Connect with me, nurture me, but don't try to hard sell me right from the start! This is the mantra of the buyer today, and they can smell an assertive hard sell from a mile away.

Buyers want to feel valued, that you are acting with integrity and a desire to help. A hard sell message out of context sticks out like a sore thumb, it's kind of uncomfortable, isn't it?

All the more reason to plan the conversation, to build your

case, but make sure there is agreement all the way through. That's always been the key to great selling.

By listening to people actively, they will buy rather than trying to force them to buy.

> *The Trusted Advisor's focus in the new world:*
> *Put the interests of your customer first, then*
> *plan the conversation, get agreement, and*
> *make rapport building your highest priority.*
> *Once there has been value recognised, then*
> *you have earned the right to ask the question.*
> *These are the key ingredients to increasing*
> *the odds of a converted sale.*

> *Selling in the New World Imperative:*
>
> *Understanding the rules of engagement*
> *with your buyers in the new world is*
> *critically important in making sure you*
> *are successful in the new era of sales.*
> *Accept that the new buying*
> *environment has changed and re-*
> *position yourself to thrive.*

Chapter 3
Re-thinking in the new world

What a unique opportunity we have been granted: to re-tool the strategy, re-tool the skills, and re-tool our mindset for success. Being able to re-calibrate your process, to re-imagine a new way of going to market, or to refine an old idea that has now become relevant leaves us open to a better way.

We talked about how the new market may have shown up where you are deficient in your tools of trade: collateral, website, social media presence, or scripting all presents an opportunity to freshen up and to re-brand.

If you are a salesperson who hasn't adapted to the new way to engage on social media and doesn't have a presence and background on delivering prolific and provocative content, you need to get to get up to speed.

The good news is that there is plenty of help available. LinkedIn has tutorials, or you can post a project on Upwork and ask for people to provide expertise in the social media space; you will be flooded by requests. This is part of the re-tooling journey: how can you be a better form of yourself?

In the 2020s and beyond, selling is all about "presenting a persuasive and compelling business case that is in the other person's self-interest to create action."

Depending upon what you sell, this could mean that the person's self-interest is a personal cause such as more wealth, more safety, or more family time. In terms of the business case, it could be one of the four business drivers that I will talk about later on in the book.

The need to create a compelling case is going to be required, especially for new business acquisition as buyers are navigating a wide range of issues and you may not be the highest priority to them when they already have a perfectly fine supplier.

The other part to this definition that becomes important is that they will buy more than ever in their self-interest, where they will have no hesitation to change from your offering if they feel unloved and unsupported.

It all starts with re-thinking what the expectations are when it comes to the new mantras of selling.

The mantras of the new world

At the core of great selling in the long term is to sell by grounded consistent values. It will add weight to your proposition when a buyer can sense that you are speaking from the heart and also standing by your promise.

Salespeople who will succeed in the next decade and beyond are those who sell by the new mantras of this new world.

Here are what I call the _Mantras of the New Selling World_:

- It's not about how we sell, _it's all about how people buy_.
- It's not about price, _it's all about how much value you give to the buyer_.
- It's not about closing the sale, _it's about making it easy for people to buy_.
- It's not about the steps of a sales call, _it's all about the levels of engagement of the customer or prospect_.
- It's not about the quantity of prospects in the pipeline or connections in social media, _it's about deep, quality referrals and introductions_.
- It's not about creating and selling trust, _it's about earning and displaying trust_.
- It's not about pushing your product or service, _it's about providing a compelling reason for them to want to walk across hot coals to get it_.
- It's not only about more and more customers, _it's about putting a nice big bear hug around your current relationships so they don't go anywhere_.
- It's not about needing more time, _it's about how you focus your efforts and make things happen_.

Re-thinking our role

Never before has the market needed Trusted Advisors more in business than right now!

When you consider that there are going to be more risk averse buyers out there for a while and the desire to do business with people they know and trust, it is the perfect time for the professional salesperson to learn the ways of the Trusted Advisor in selling.

Our role is to be insightful about the market and trends ahead, to understand that our end goal for all client relationships is to attract the prospect, nurture, and convert into a client and then to continue to expand the relationship.

There are degrees to being a Trusted Advisor depending on what you're selling and how complex a sale is. But I wouldn't always call a customer service person or a retail sales person a "Trusted Advisor" unless there are longer conversations and recommendations sought. Doing what you say you will, acting with transparency and honesty, and following up are core characteristics that make me a Trusted Advisor in my business. Those are the things that changed my career.

Have they given me more confidence in what I do? Absolutely. Have they given me more self-esteem? Absolutely.

We need to "re-tool" in this new market by getting better at the how rather than just bombarding people and badgering them into the sale.

We need to recognise a qualified buyer from one who is just being polite and not hounding the buyer until they just "don't take no for an answer." That just not going to cut it.

Do they have available funds to buy from you? Do they have a current contract that doesn't allow them to move from the incumbent? I talk a great deal in this book about referrals and introductions, which to me is always the smartest way to make sales. The sales process is shorter and converts at a much higher rate.

Cold calling without warming up the opportunity is just plain stupid. We are in the conversion business and not just activity. So why not think about how you can work less in terms of sweat equity and think more in terms of strategic thinking?

Part 2

RUNNING YOUR BUSINESS INSIDE THE BUSINESS

It all starts with you as the autonomous Trusted Advisor.

Chapter 4
It all starts with you!

So what do these changes in the new world mean to the selling profession and how do we as Trusted Advisors make sure we are well positioned to be relevant and resilient in this new selling world?

A concept I have spoken about in my workshops over the years is the "business within the business concept." To frame this up for you, I have always believed that we ultimately run our business inside the business we promote to the market and thus determine our own pay cheque.

The successful salesperson in the new world takes responsibility for their circumstances and runs more and more autonomously. They operate from anywhere and are responsible for their professional mindset and their return on hours invested.

We all need to surround ourselves with positive stimuli, things that get us in the zone and keep us there. For some salespeople, it's as simple as upbeat music, or perhaps reading an interesting blog or article on the latest on selling or changes to your industry.

The more I work in sales and with salespeople and sales managers, the more I acknowledge that one of the great success factors in being the Trusted Advisor is your ability to be resourceful and to protect the mojo.

Fragile confidence

Confidence is everything in selling; whether you think you can or you can't, you're right!

Fragile confidence is when you fall back into negative self-talk after a challenging time. All salespeople I have met go through it at some time in their career.

So what can create a fragile confidence in sales?

- A period of slow opportunities in your pipeline
- Changing industry and having to learn all over again
- When you are creating a strong pipeline but then not confirming any business
- When your buddies in your team are converting business but you are not
- When you have lost a significant account that amounts to, say, 20 percent plus of your total budget
- When you have received a spray from a customer or your boss!

When things are going well we feel bulletproof, like nothing can get in our way. We have a product or service the market wants and needs, we are closing out opportunities, and referrals are coming in without even asking for them.

The key is to tap back into that feeling by knowing what mindset you need to have, to model the behaviours that got you there the first time.

I believe in modelling excellence, finding out what the best do and then deconstructing it so you can understand it and then create your own model. Great salespeople reflect on what made them great all the time so they can then get back into that zone and repeat it, like a professional sportsperson.

Can control, can't control, must control

I have always found it really helpful in my sales career to understand those things that I can't do anything about versus those things that I have direct control over to make sure I have the right perspective on selling.

Try this: take a piece of paper and divide the paper into three vertical columns.

In the first column, write the heading *"Can't Control."* Write down all the things you can think of that you have no control over. Things such as the economy, the weather, perhaps the strategy of the business you represent, if you are not in a decision-making position.

Now move to the second column and write *"Can Control."* Make a note of all the things that you can control. Things such as your attitude, your ability to keep in contact with your customers, your message to market, the way you manage your time.

In the last column, it's time to get really empowering. The column heading is *"Must Control."* In this column, you make a note of all the things that you know is now a priority to control from a mindset stance to succeed in sales.

Examples might be making 10 phone calls a day, organising five face-to-face meetings with new buyers each week, or perhaps to retain 85 percent of all recurring income in your established accounts.

When you have done the exercise, it will provide for you a short list of very specific things you know you must control and place a priority on.

I met an inspiring speaker many years ago by the name of W Mitchell. His book, *It's Not What Happens To You, It's What You Do About It*, is a great read.

His story is certainly a motivational one, given the adversity he has faced in his life.

Mitchell in his twenties was a vibrant man taking on the world. He loved to go out on his motorbike and experience the fullness of life.

He talks in his book about some turning points in his life that would change things forever. For example, when he was riding his motorbike in 1971 and crashed into a laundry truck on a lovely San Francisco day. Not only did he crack his pelvis and crush his left elbow, but a lid on the gas tank of his bike popped open and gasoline poured onto the hot engine and Mitchell.

He caught fire and was put out with a fire extinguisher by a man who worked at the local auto lot. In his words, he was judged to be at the "low end of survivability."

After having burns to 65 percent of his body, you would think this would be bad enough.

Mitchell was also an avid pilot, and in 1975, he crashed his Cessna and ended up paralysed. He was confined to a wheelchair from that day forward.

And… you think you are having a bad day!

He really had plenty he could be angry about in life; the thing is, when you meet the guy and chat with him, he is positive and really charismatic. His whole talk is about is the difference is in your reaction, the decisions you make in response to the environment, and the cards you are dealt.

As Mitchell says, "Take responsibility for your future."

Getting leverage on yourself

Creating your own **mastermind group** of positive thinkers who will expect more of you than you expect of yourself is a critical way to get leverage on yourself.

You could meet as a group over breakfast once every month

or quarter to compare how you are all doing but also give permission to the group to keep yourself accountable to them.

If your purpose is purely to create new opportunities or leads, then consider forming the referral club where the express purpose is to make sure you are living the rules of reciprocation and setting each other up with email handshakes or phone introductions.

If it is better for you to work one to one, then consider an **accountability buddy** to maintain the focus. This also becomes easy to arrange. Being accountable to someone means that you now have a bigger reason to do something.

Make a commitment to be future focused and talk about how you will achieve something by a certain time. Then give permission to that person to check in on how you are progressing.

Permission is the key; let them know you have standard excuses why you can't do something and let them know they can call BS on it. Trust is the foundation stone, the glue that holds it all together. You will be more honest with someone whom you know has your interests at heart.

Being positive in your conversations is also critical. There are enough people out there who will tell you what can't be done in the world and how things aren't great.

Choose a different path.

Be selective with your social media use as it can be destructive to your selling resilience. Social media is a place where you can find yourself questioning your circumstances and also falling into the comparison trap.

Choose which media you will listen to, which you will participate in, and know when it is mission critical to turn it off so you can clearly think about your own journey and plan the journey.

Chapter 5
Getting a good return on your time!

Time is money in the new world.

I guess you could say in selling it's always been the law of high performance; however, with companies hiring at different speeds, sales teams will be stretched to get more done in less time.

There are certain philosophical beliefs I have found Trusted Advisors have about time management and how we get the most out of efforts:

- It's amazing what you can get done in one day and amazing what you can<u>not</u> get done in one day!

- We all have the same 1,440 minutes in each day; it's about how we use them!

- There is no such thing as time management anyway. It's really about how we manage ourselves.

- It's got a lot to do with how we see our ability to take control.
- It's a reflection of the decisions we make—or don't make!
- You need to have a plan and to work the plan.
- Get proactively get ahead of the problem before it grows to be out of hand.
- Understand how important it is to create the perception of being ultra-responsive with the customer (more about that later).

The power of clarity

Getting really clear on what you want, when you want it, and how you are going to get it are critical to your ability to making sure your goals are in alignment and your time is apportioned the smart way.

Dreaming big is a part of the process and so is making the dreams or big hairy audacious goals (BHAGs as Jim Collins calls them in *Good to Great*) a reality. There's not much equity in an idea if you don't implement it and make it a tangible achievement.

Clarity for salespeople is to focus on **three main goals.** This has always been a big part of my sales professionals' sales plan where we plan out the three goals and add to it the tactical and implementation plans to make it happen.

Think now of what your **money making activities are -**

those things that you know will help you to sell more and create more income.

Things like maximizing more face-to-face time in front of a qualified referred buyer, preparing the presentation in advance or increasing your conversion rate by being in sync with your buyer.

Revenue producing time is like gold. When the fish are biting, we need to give it the maximum attention and also working the standard 9 to 5 day goes out the window in place of confirmed business.

I knew a financial planner many years ago who always said that he was unavailable in May and June to catch up for lunch as this was when he made his money for the year. Reminds me of the diary business; we made 83 percent of our sales in 16 weeks a year.

Thinking that planning doesn't matter because you'll always "wind up where you are supposed to go" is like firing an arrow in any direction and claiming the target is wherever it hits. Salespeople who live like that are a passive force, turning and twisting with every new shiny object, relevant or not.

My first introduction to time management as a concept was via a workshop in the 1980s by Dr. Time: Alec Mackenzie.

Dr. Mackenzie released his book *The Time Trap* in 1973 and it drew a lot of attention as a reasonable, though perhaps slightly fussy, approach to getting a lot done in one day. Mackenzie suggested that to manage time, the first thing you need to do is to keep a time log.

A few things still stand out for me about what he shared in this workshop (not bad when you consider it was over 30 years ago!).

The power of a to-do list, the 80/20 rule, and the power of clarity of your goals are things I still talk about today with the salespeople and sales managers I work with.

He was one of the first people to commercialise time management as a personal development subject and had a time management system he had designed which I was looking at for our range.

When you run your business inside the business and you really embrace the concept, you know there is one commodity more precious than any other: <u>time</u>.

So what are the most common ways I see salespeople potentially squandering time?

Here are some common ones:

1. *Working on proposals that don't go ahead.*

    We don't always know if they won't go ahead, but sometimes we waste big time on small opportunities.

2. *Spending time with "nibblers" who run you around in circles.*

    There are people who just need more and more information to do more and more research, with no impending result.

3. *Time to get to meetings and managing their territory.*

There are salespeople who manage their territory and customer run really well and there are those who don't.

4. *Servicing business and farming disproportionately to their hunting efforts.*

     Where business is looked after by the account service team, keep out of it.

5. *Not creating new processes, templates, and systems.*

     Trusted Advisor Selling is all about evolving as a salesperson. That means getting better and more streamlined in our approach.

The decisions you make

As a Trusted Advisor who is focused on being a high performer, there are a number of decisions you make to maximise the output in each week.

Decision #1: Make a decision to be proactive and see problems before they occur.

Decision #2: Control your day before it controls you, put in not negotiables.

Decision #3: Finish the week before it starts, plan what an ideal week looks like.

Decision #4: Make sandwich calls on every sales call; visit a new company each side of the appointment you have made and introduce yourself. That could add up to 40 or more new prospects a month!

Decision #5: The 60/15 principle—the goal of achieving 60 percent of your budget by the 15th of the month.

Decision #6: Learn to say no; think about which things you agree to and which ones are a big imposition on your time.

Decision #7: Create more powerful and time saving processes and systems, like standard form proposals.

One percenters to maximising your time

If you pick up any good time management book, you will find a ton of great little ways to get the edge and save time in your day. Create a thirst for time saving and maximizing your selling opportunity.

Here is a list of some things that have helped me to keep the focus:

- Streamlining by creating macros on the computer
- Speed reading
- Multi-tasking
- Taking regular breaks
- Having 90-minute focus sessions
- Working to your peak energy periods
- Drinking plenty of water (still a work in progress!)
- Using email sorting software
- Defining periods for social media updates
- Turning off my notifications

- Starting the week on Sunday night to get a jump on the week
- Learning to say no—don't over commit
- Completing the hardest task first—it sets the day up for success
- Asking myself, "What's the best use of my time right now?"
- Re-confirming meetings in advance assumptively
- Planning the next day's schedule the night before
- Keeping a clean desk at the end of the day
- Holding as many stand-up meetings with colleagues as possible instead of sitting in the meeting room
- Selecting clothes and ironing shirt the night before

Chapter 6
Being mobile and autonomous

The new selling world will see more and more questioning as to whether businesses need to have the bricks and mortar they always did.

A great client of mine has a national sales force and they have now chosen to close down the field offices for the organisation and have the team operating from home. They will gladly pay for the salespeople to use a shared office facility.

This is the way of the world now. Why pay for an office which is hardly used? Let's face it, as a sales manager, you don't want the team working from their desk all the time. You want them out in the field doing their job!

Salespeople like to get together; it's part of the gregarious nature of salespeople. So can we have both? The autonomous nature of working outside the office whilst still getting together?

I think the new selling world will not only allow for it, it will be a competitive advantage and make you an employer of choice if you promote it.

Hot seating and work hubs

The great thing about the mobile world and hot seating is that you only pay for what you use. Don't want the meeting room? No problem, you don't need to pay for it unless you use it. Use it for an hour and pay for an hour. Need some copying done or scanning of some documents? Great, just pay per page.

In my building in Melbourne, small business operators consistently run meetings and work on their laptops in the food court.

My brother was area manager for a beer brand in Canada and he worked from home most of the time, turning up at the office for the occasional meeting. It worked well. So many people in recent times have even found they have a preference to working from home!

Sales managers who require salespeople to turn up first thing in the morning, then leave from the office at the end of the day rather than leaving from their last appointment are not providing the flexibility to work from where the salespeople can be productive. Those management styles are fast disappearing.

Change the rules: it's all about results.

Having a weekly catch up with your fellow sales team in the centrally positioned coffee shop makes sense. Make it an opportunity to catch up and share war stories, whilst at the same time have the serious bit where we all have to report the KPIs against the company budget.

Every salesperson can take the responsibility of choosing a new venue, moving the meeting spot around. What a great way to keep things fresh.

On a number of occasions in my early days in this business, I delivered training to a team when they hired a back function room at a local café. So many of them have meeting rooms, and remember the weekly trade from the local mothers' group is pretty good.

Managing by KPI's

The new world requires rethinking of how we get the most of our role while at the same time providing flexibility.

During the pandemic where many were not able to go to the office if they were not an essential service, we just coped. Salespeople still made the calls, still served their customers, and still held sales meetings via Zoom.

The question is, what can we take away from the world where we had no choice to now where we can craft our workplace and look at output rather than old paradigms?

Perhaps the onus has shifted for sales leaders to think of ways we manage by clearly defined KPIs that can be reported on so everyone gets what they need to do their role.

Being autonomous and working from a range of locations - being a truly mobile office - is not for everyone and we have seen this already.

Selling in the New World Imperative:

The rules of engagement for sales teams have shifted. Flexibility is the key, and for the business owner, it may just save you a few bucks in rent you don't need to shell out.

Part 3

BEING OF SERVICE FIRST

Buyers need to know you care before you ask for their business.

Chapter 7
Mastering the fine line

Clients need to know that we truly care. Not just for the benefit of making the quick order, but because they are people just like us.

This was loud and clear during the COVID-19 crisis where people in sales just reached out to other people. It wasn't the time to sell in the traditional sense, to present your message and to ask for the business.

People needed to feel secure, that they could trust you and rely on the promises you have made. A call to just ask "how are you?" is appreciated, and the business will follow.

The new selling world is a place where we believe in the spirit of service.

The fine line

The fine line in selling in the new world is to reach out to clients and be of service, earning the right to ask for the business.

When you care and you go the extra mile to help, you then earn the right to ask for more business and to ask for referrals and introductions to build your business.

We need to be givers, to care and to serve with heart. Anything less will make you irrelevant. Embrace the qualities of sincerity, understanding, generosity, connectivity, and credibility.

The amazing thing about giving is that you actually feel better by being generous and reaching out to others, and it comes back in spades.

A generous spirit in sales will make people notice and want to be around you. Patience with decision making and understanding of your buyer in an uncertain time will make you stand out.

Be kind and you will be happy

I recently interviewed a good friend of mine, Mr. Ken Keis, President of CRG in Canada, who is one of the world leaders in profiling tools, about kindness and happiness.

He talked at the interview about how kindness has a multiplying effect and how when you are kind to someone there is elevation where others help each other.

Like going to the local coffee shop and you "pay it forward" by paying for the coffee of the next person or like one coffee shop owner near where we live who started a sticky note system where you pay for a coffee and write it on a sticky note. You then leave it on the board for when someone who needs the coffee and money is tight can then take a sticky note.

Ken made the point that there was a study done by Gallop of over 142 countries that asked about engagement levels of employees in companies all around the world. No surprise: 87 percent of the world's population were to some point disengaged at work.

Very few people actually do what they like and enjoy. Purpose is everything.

Nothing happens by accident, intentionality is the key. There are no accidents. When you tap into your purpose, work never seems like work. Keep journaling each day and the answers will become clearer to you.

The 5 qualities you must have

The new world of selling demands that we be of service to our clients, to be connected to them, to their successes and challenges. When you sell with heart, you sell on a different level.

Sincerity

The heart of the sale.

Don't underestimate the power of being in total sync with your customer by genuinely caring about their situation. People will remember how much you cared when they needed extended payment terms, a better price to take upstairs, or delivery outside the normal terms of trade. Be present and find out about them on a different level. Invest in the relationship and actually care, and you will find that it will multiply.

I was a Dale Carnegie course instructor for close to eight years. You will know the Dale Carnegie name from the classic book, *How to Win Friends and Influence People.*

After graduating from being a participant in the program, I was offered the opportunity to embark on an intensive training program to become a course instructor.

Teaching the course in my early 20s was a transformational experience for me, and there are certain principles about human relations I still consider critical to good selling.

One of Carnegie's principles from his best-selling book was "don't criticise, condemn, or complain."

For salespeople it could mean:

- Don't criticise your competition,
- Don't condemn anybody, and
- Don't complain about the company you work for (I've seen that!).

Great human relations never go away, we just get lazy in sales. Get sincerely involved, listen, and put yourself in the buyer's position.

Understanding

The rules have changed and this requires more emotional

intelligence, to fully be present and look for the signs.

A client now may have a smaller team working a lot more hours. They may need you to provide more evidence of your business case, all designed to get approval moving forward.

A client may need you to get back to them with regular reporting on stockholdings, or to come in and show the team how to sell your product as a reseller. Do it.

In selling, I think it's too easy not to really want to understand where the buyer is at. Perhaps we haven't asked enough questions to fully explore the situation?

Patience is what will be required to building for the long term and not just for the quick buck.

Generosity

My dad always said that good business was all about giving people "more than they expected." It's funny, my son has just applied for his first part-time job and I gave him the same advice.

If you are willing to be more generous with your customer, you will find ways where you can continually add value. It might be an email where you were reflecting on a conversation the two of you had last week or as simple as saving them some freight charges by dropping by.

Send them an article which talks about something of interest to them and gives the client some ideas. Do you think you might be memorable to them now?

It is out of the attitude of serving that sales will happen. Some would say you need to give to get. In the new market you need to give in buckets.

Credibility

Your reputation has become more critical than ever before. One of our discussions in this book is to be able to collaborate with others and to create more referrals and introductions. Without a really fine reputation, this is hard to achieve.

You are always on show in sales and it hardly seems fair that you can do everything right year after year and yet drop the ball once and then the buyer questions your ability to serve them. That's sales. I could have made integrity the sixth quality, but I think it fits well here. Integrity is doing what is right and not what is easy. It's acting with character and being reliable.

Do a little more, make sure the buyer recognises it, and then make sure you capture the reputation in the form of testimonials.

Connectivity

Being available is all part of the new world of selling: connected and responsive.

Being "At Your Service" means people can connect with you easily as a salesperson. There should be a number of ways they can reach you whether it be SMS, phone, email, Facebook, Messenger, LinkedIn message and for you to be regularly checking the mediums to see if there is a call required.

Amaze the buyer with your responsiveness. As a Trusted Advisor, it's all about being alert to the market and then delivering beyond their expectation. Under-promise and over-deliver.

Chapter 8
The likeability factor

Let's face it, some people in sales make it so hard to do business. They complicate the sale, they don't get back to you, they have that sourpuss look on their face, or they complain about the lack of leads or the economy being down.

These salespeople will be the ones who will disappear from the market; they are not cut out to serve. Selling is all about making yourself easy to buy. So how do we make ourselves more likeable, more magnetic so we can create more opportunities and convert the ones we have?

10 Ways to increase likeability

Be Curious

The buyer has invited you into his or her space. It could be workspace, the corner of a shop, an office, or a home office.

Curiosity questions get the prospect talking about their passions, and whatever they say is packed with information about their real selves. Be curious. Be attentive. Be a great learner. Paraphrase and repeat back to the buyer your understanding; you will be amazed at the increase in rapport.

Be Unambiguous

Being unambiguous lets clients know where they stand, and knowing that builds confidence, which should evolve into trust. In business-to-business selling, the meeting is frequently held on their turf. In other kinds of selling, the meeting is more often held on yours. If you don't know the answer, don't make stuff up. If delivery needs to be Thursday, it's Thursday. If you can beat that, great. As my dad always said, "Under-promise and over-deliver."

Be positive, happy, and energetic

If you can make someone laugh, I think you are halfway there! Being positive, happy, and energetic makes you more attractive. On a tough day, if you need to take a minute in the car before you go in to see the client, then do it. Get the frame of mind right and remember this moment of truth with the client is too important not to be "on."

Be proud and purposeful

To make a confident sale, you've got to be proud of yourself, your company, and your product.

Being proud of your product can be settled by focusing on what's special about it. Is yours the fastest? The most effective?

The smartest? The most stylish? Or even the cheapest? You've got to stand for something. Knowing what you stand for creates pride. Let them know that you are fortunate to serve them and to work for the company you represent.

Be easy to deal with

Being easy to deal with is all part of your professionalism. Don't make buyers feel they're an imposition. Don't make any aspect of the sales process hard.

Everybody hates a hassle (and a hustle). Have everything on hand, make it easy for them to pay, and use words like "sure," "okay," and "you bet" as often as possible. You may have to go the extra mile to iron out trouble spots beforehand, but that's all part of sales preparation.

Be thankful

Thank your client for their business. Do something a little bit extra, something they don't expect. Send them an article about whatever was under discussion, a generic piece about, say, "the art of management" or something else that is pertinent to your conversation.

If they've bought a printer from you, give them a free ream of paper to get them started. If they've bought a coffee, give them a customer rewards card. It doesn't have to cost much; just a small reminder that you're grateful for their business. Everybody loves a "thank you." I bet your competitor doesn't bother saying thanks.

Be responsive

Customers like and trust salespeople who are responsive to their needs. It makes them feel important, as if they matter after the selling business is over. Being quick, responsive and enthusiastic is a matter of attitude. And it doesn't necessarily have to cost a cent. It makes you memorable and puts you ahead of the pack. Over-deliver in responsiveness as well as product.

Be reliable

Buyers don't trust unreliable people. Why should they? Show them you're reliable by living up to your promises and ensuring your product does the same. Don't exaggerate your product's capabilities or your ability to deliver on schedule. Stay the course. Live up to your promises. Be a phone call away when your buyer has a query. Pick up the phone and show you have the buyer's best interests at heart. Be punctual; there is no excuse for being late to client meetings.

Be referable

Taking care of all the above will make you likeable and trustworthy. Make the effort to check your customers' satisfaction levels. If they're displeased, fix it. And if they're pleased, let the dust settle, then pop the question: will your customer refer you to others? Likeable people get referrals, and if you live up to your billing, it makes the referrer look good.

My dad always said, "Use your ears and mouth in the right proportion." We've got to be great listeners. Listening means active listening. If you listen attentively, you'll never make the mistake of talking over the top of buying cues. When the customer brings something up, stick with that line rather than whatever you've got in your briefcase.

Some salespeople are so programmed to parrot out their spiel that they stick with it at all costs. Wrong. Our job is to make a sale, not to faithfully deliver whatever they've been taught to say. When we do that, there goes all rapport.

Here's an example of a missed cue: I accompanied a young woman named Kirsten who was new at selling mobile phones and data plans. I was her coach, but the buyer didn't care why I was there - he didn't even ask for my business card. Kirsten chatted away about what she had to offer, which was a sizeable opportunity and the buyer went straight to page 17 of the proposal, looked at the numbers, got his calculator out, and started working out the savings.

That was all he was worried about. Meanwhile, Kirsten was back on page 2, talking about the background to the company and all the different products they had to offer, while he was working out the figures right in front of her eyes.

I thought, *She's going to miss this opportunity, so I jumped in and said,* "I couldn't help but notice you've gone straight to the investment page. May I ask what was it you were looking for in terms of the savings to move to us?"

He said, "I was looking at saving a grand a month."

I said, "I can see from Kirsten's proposal that the saving is $900 per month. If that's correct, is there any reason why you wouldn't go ahead?"

He said, "I think I can sell this upstairs."

Meanwhile, Kirsten hadn't paid any attention to our conversation. She went straight back to page 2 and said, "I just want to talk about the different models of phones available…". I'm thinking, *This person wants to talk about the money and not about phones, you're missing this whole buying signal!*

Selling in the New World Imperative:

We always talked in my early sales days about being in rapport with your customer. The new world asks us to consider how we can be more likeable and in tune with our customer. Then you become someone they want to be around and this builds the relationship.

Chapter 9
We are <u>all</u> in the business of selling

Organisations that understand that the whole enterprise is in sales and not just the field sales team will be the ones that thrive in the new world.

We have already mentioned that the cost of new client acquisition in many industries is on the rise. With that in mind, the lowest hanging fruit in any business is the incoming enquiry that already exists; every client phone call, email, and visit from an existing client is a sales opportunity.

If you have been part of a silo business in the past with each department just focusing on their own outputs without considering the greater good, you will know how it is giving away a key area of competitive advantage. Silo thinking is easy to observe as a consultant.

People just going about their daily tasks and perhaps even playing the blame game where the language is centred on "them and they" rather than "we."

When I interviewed Troy Eadie from Business Success Systems in my NewSelling weekly podcast program, he put it beautifully: "A holistic view puts a moat around the business!"

The magnetic business

Sales teams who can collaborate with their other departments and provide a consistent united front will win in this new market.

The strategic salesperson who can enlist the help of a service advisor or customer service representative creates incremental opportunities.

A buyer is always attracted to a business where the team members:

- Look like they are happy to work there
- Take pride in their work to get things right
- Follow up to make sure you are happy
- Have each other's back and won't criticize each other
- Enjoy their work and have fun but not to take attention away from the customer
- Take any feedback as a learning experience and don't become defensive the moment a suggestion is made
- Don't rush out the door at 5:01 p.m. and leave the reception area unattended
- Take pride in the cleanliness and neatness of the place

Working in truck sales extensively over the last six years, there is a saying when we talk about creating a dynamic sales culture.

"Sales makes the first sale, but service and parts make the next one and the next one…"

It's true, the service and parts teams will have more contact with the customer than the sales team after the sale has been made. This relationship is leverageable.

What are some of the easy to spot differences of an organisation that lives and breathes this dynamic sales culture?

- A common goal and purpose
- A commitment to work as a team
- A commitment to constant and never-ending improvement
- Agreed rules of engagement – i.e., the old three-rings policy for incoming phone calls
- Cross departmental meetings so everyone knows what is going on
- Clear vision and mission communicated
- Great induction program and cross-trained staff

It starts with values

Focusing in on the core values of the team provides the foundation to a great sales team and broader single enterprise team. Which of these values applies to you and your team?

Accountability

Excellence

Competitive

Trust

Commitment

Honesty

Reliability

Generosity

Creativity

Self-discipline

Compassion

Patience

Respect

Success

Ethics

Toughness

Balance

There are plenty of others you can put on the list, but this provides a starting point. Zero in on, say, three or four as a team and then build from there. Great values agreed to by the whole organisation are powerful in creating the "we are all in the business of selling" mindset. Not only will it galvanise the team and provide a bear hug around your client base that others will not be able to penetrate, you can proudly market this difference from your competitors.

Now you have some agreed values with the team; what are the underlying behaviours that would be representative of these values?

This is where the rubber hits the road. Being able to brainstorm all the ways that you currently provide evidence to the foundations of these values. Perhaps it's the ability to get back to people quickly, the ability to cover for other team members, or your attitude towards walking your talk.

So how would you measure these behaviours?

Let's say one of your values in the team is **integrity** and the behaviour that supports that is the commitment made by the team of "walking your talk" by always getting back to the customer. The next obvious question is - by when?

Measurements of success now really make the behaviour come to life - is it within the hour, same day, next day? Create a scorecard as a team. Then score yourself against these numbers, and you now have an accountable team committed to sales growth of the company.

The market wants it fast, real fast.

Circumstances may prevent you from competing on price, distribution, location, or even quality. But you can always compete on speed, if you choose to.

A fast response used to be "exception service." It has gone from being a virtue to an expectation. Business is speeding up. Quick response is now an essential characteristic of the single enterprise team.

When I started in sales, the fax machine was the fastest way to get something to the customer. Salespeople would come in off the road, prepare their fax, and hope to have a clear line to get the fax out. Then - hey, presto! It would spit out of the buyer's fax machine at the receiving end. Salespeople who said they could get a faxed reply on the same day were impressive!

We now have the ability to send a document while talking with the buyer, so there is no downtime in between defining moments in the sales process.

Some customers don't push as much as others about cost; they'll pay a premium for speed. So are you being as magnetic as possible as a Trusted Advisor in the market?

How about the sales team around you? Have you committed to be the best in the industry and to set new benchmarks that make you different from your competitors?

The new world also wants this goal to be a company-wide ideal, where every contact I have with your organisation, you get me, respect me, and value me.

Part 4

SELLING LIKE THE TRUSTED ADVISOR

Master these five areas and you will be relevant and bulletproof

Chapter 10
How to sell like the Trusted Advisor!

Buyers are crying out for people who can make their life easier, save them time, and provide real recommendations. Since I have been talking about being the Trusted Advisor in sales, I thought it would now be time to define the total concept.

Being a Trusted Advisor will make you a magnet to referrals, it will allow you to make more margin as there is less price conversation, and it helps you to leverage an industry expert positioning.

When you are a Trusted Advisor, you are a sounding board and trusted partner in their business where they ask for your opinion and also ask for help in sourcing other products and services they require.

So what makes a Trusted Advisor? How do they operate, what are their traits, and can we create a model that can be replicated?

- Trusted Advisors are in the business of *transforming* the customer experience and not just being *transactional.*
- Trusted Advisors partner with clients and see *ongoing business* as being the currency of their success.
- Trusted Advisors have solid values at their core of their selling and are authentic: "If I don't know the answer, I will find out."
- Trusted Advisors are real, they believe in the value of a *promise.*
- Trusted Advisors are *ambassadors* for their company brand and understand the power of a personal brand.
- Trusted Advisors are prepared for the sales call and *proactive* in moving when the buyer moves.
- Trusted Advisors are *relevant;* they read widely, understand changes in their market, and have good competitor intelligence.
- Trusted Advisors *put their focus on the buyer* and are fully present with the client so they will pick up things others won't. This focus lets them identify real needs and strong emotional wants.
- Trusted Advisors *sell premium* and bulletproof themselves with research to build a price justification argument on the difference between their solution and the low-cost competitor.

- Trusted Advisors make a discernment about where *they spend their time* (high value versus low value accounts, and high and low maintenance accounts), this allows them to hit their numbers.

- Trusted Advisors understand the *value of theatre* and how it plays a role in the confirmed sale.

- Trusted Advisors "*own their numbers*"; they reverse-engineer their sales budget, break it down into bite-size chunks, and then go after it with fervour.

- Trusted Advisors will always look for the *referral* opportunity over the cold appointment. They have done the numbers, know their conversion rates, and want the best chance of success.

- Trusted Advisors *ask great questions* and don't spend the whole appointment telling the prospect how wonderful they and their company are.

Being the authority

Do you have something to say? Is your market listening?

In the new selling world, to be the Trusted Advisor, you need to be able to prove your case, to build an argument by designing models and process visuals that give people your view of the world. Salespeople who simply provide fact and benefit statements will be left behind as a "me too." Customers want insight, opinion, and things they can't just download - to be the trusted authority.

Being prolific in posting ideas, solutions, and deep thinking in response to client challenges will be the key to developing a reputation. Being provocative in how you present the thinking and take a contrarian view will make you stand out.

So, to call yourself an *authority,* what do you need to have as traits?

1. *A genuine curiosity* about the product, the solution, and being the problem solver. It starts with accepting a new role in the induction period, asking questions, and noting the most common questions you will get.

2. An increasing *body of work and knowledge.* If you are a service provider, this might mean the latest research and being able to speak with confidence as you read widely. Product solution salespeople need to know add-ons, product variations, colours, sizes, models, and how to create a customised solution.

3. *An ability to transfer complicated information into easily understood chunks.* The authority creates pictures and examples that make the body of knowledge instantly recognisable through a simple visual.

Developing your own intellectual property

I recently interviewed Chad Barr from the Chad Barr Group for my NewSelling Program, an authority in helping entrepreneurs to create digital empires.

In the interview, he mentioned that developing good intellectual property in the market is just about a number of simple steps to get started on the journey to being someone who can package your ideas.

Ask yourself:

What is one of the *biggest challenges* my target market encounters?

Make a list and then take one in particular to go deeper. For me, it would be salespeople not getting referrals and introductions from clients due to their own mindset.

Now think to yourself, what are the *three best ways* to solve the problem for the buyer?

Going back to my example, it would be mindset, not having a clear process to do it, and mastering the language to ask for referrals.

The secret is now to create a process to make this piece of content come to life.

Now once you have brainstormed the answers to these critical questions, talk down the camera and capture this as a case study, talking about how your customers have these problems.

One of the most powerful ways to make this have enormous credibility is to talk in the *third person:*

"One of my clients said to me just yesterday that one of the biggest challenges they face is…"

The opportunity is to then start to create ways of

transferring these ideas to products that position you, such as:

- An ebook or special report, around four to five pages only would be okay.
- A magalogue – a combination of catalogue about your services combined with magazine articles, so it looks like a glossy magazine off the rack.
- Conversation topics relevant to your industry that you can post and ask for feedback.
- General quotes that you can post to give people a glimpse of how you see the world (be careful with political comment or current affairs).
- A printed quality book, if you sell services.
- Process visuals to show a framework for your unique processes.

The Trusted Advisors key traits

The Trusted Advisor in selling can be best described in a nutshell as being someone who pays attention to these key areas:

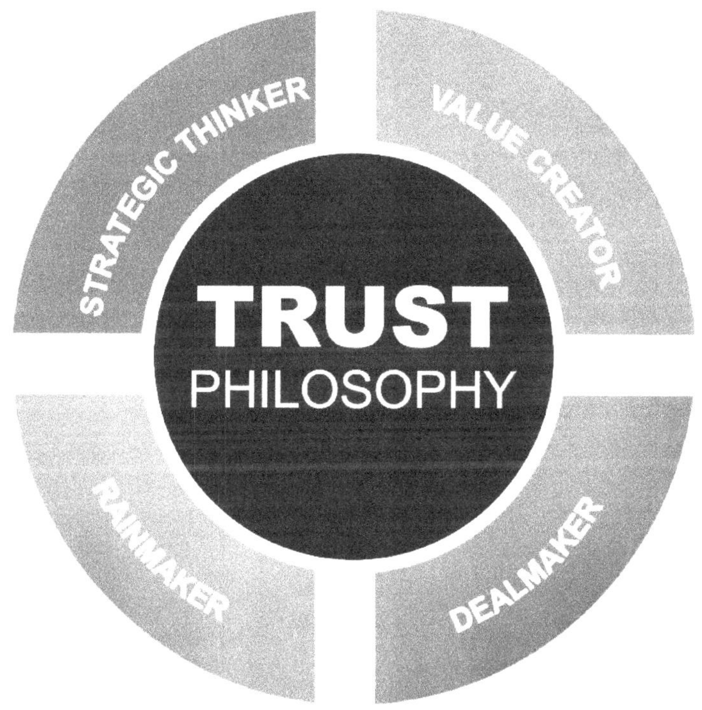

The Strategic Thinker – how to work smarter and not harder.

The Value Creator – knowing what drives the customer and making sure we value add all the time.

The Deal Maker – getting the numbers and converting the opportunities.

The Rain Maker – creating multiple streams of opportunities.

The Trust Maker – the glue that binds, creating the lifetime reputation.

In this section to selling in the new world, I go into each area and give you a snapshot of what you need to master to be the true Trusted Advisor in sales.

Selling in the New World Imperative:

The Trusted Advisor positioning in the market has real advantages: better conversion, deeper relationships, and more referrals. Stand apart and reap the rewards!

Chapter 11
The Strategic Thinker

As a Strategic Thinker, you understand the critical sales numbers and the determinants of how you will achieve your budget.

Tracking and measuring your results with a *think smarter and not work harder* mindset means you get real leverage on your time.

Know your critical numbers

Critical numbers are the numbers you should know because they are a measure of how you're travelling. You own these numbers. They tell you where you should focus your energies, whom you should be talking to and what you should be doing next.

Critical numbers are usually activity-based, like how many calls you make per day, how many appointments per week, or how many knocks on doors.

These and their results are all critical numbers.

You've got to know what you're currently doing. If I produce $500,000 per year in sales revenue at a high margin and my sales manager says, "I want you to do $650,000 this year," (which is not unusual) how will you get the extra?

You might happen to get a 10 to 15 percent increase in sales for the year because the market's good from your current base. Where are you getting the rest from? This is what I call *the strategic gap*.

Your <u>strategic gap</u> is very simple:
- Where you want to be
- Where you are today
- What you can budget for in terms of organic growth?
- What's the gap you now need to generate of new business?
- What action you have to take to fill that gap?

When you reverse engineer your sales budget, everything changes. You start to think of what needs to happen to cover the spread rather than trying to think of how you are going to possibly move your achieved sales by 10 to 20 percent for the next year. So why not develop a strategy?

Sit down and work out precisely how you're going to get that $650,000? There's no point leaving it until the 11th month and going, *Oh crap! I'm not going to get my sales budget!*

Now think of the critical numbers in your budget right now and start by getting to work.

List:

- Number of individual sales you have made in the last 12 months?
- How many customers you've added this year?
- How many times on average each customer purchased from you?
- The average spend per customer?
- Gross margin per sale?
- What bundles you sold?
- Your conversion rate from a company generated lead?
- Your conversion rate from self-generated efforts?
- Retention rate of key customers?
- Length of time to move someone through the selling cycle?
- Number of prospects in the pipeline and amount of sales they may represent?
- The 80/20 Rule: what does your top 20 percent of customers represent in terms of total sales in your sales budget?

Create a scorecard for you and only you. In one column, pop in what you will measure, the next column your current performance, and the third column to contain your goal measurement.

The Trusted Advisor's one-page plan

Very few salespeople have anything resembling a sales plan. I mean key strategies, a tactical plan to achieve those strategies, and some quantifiable actions to achieve the tactics that can be part of your weekly activities.

The Strategic Thinker creates a one-page sales plan each year and then updates it quarterly to the changing conditions.

They are the first ones to recognise when they are not performing in this plan at the required standard and will adjust accordingly, getting to the sales manager before the manager gets to them.

Start with an overarching goal of what you would like the year to look like.

What is the sales growth you are aiming for and is it realistic based on previous year achievements and opportunities you are seeing out there?

Is a 20 percent increase in sales reasonable based on what you are seeing? How about a 10 percent increase in a tough market where you know it's actually contracting and you need to hold on to your existing customers like crazy?

Now get to work on the four tactical areas that will make that a reality.

Here are some of the most common areas I work on when I do one-to-one coaching with a sales professional:-

Section 1 – Your individual sales target

Do the numbers:

- Sales to be achieved from current accounts

- Sales required to be achieved from organic growth
- Sales required as new business from new accounts
- Sales opportunities from lapsed or dormant accounts

Breaking the budget down into bite-sized chunks of quarters and then months and weeks helps to keep the focus on getting the number.

Section 2 – Marketing effort required

In this section, make a commitment to what marketing activities you are going to commit to over the planning period that will support your sales budget goals in Section 1:

- Outbound new business activities
- CRM activities to reactivate and drive new business
- New collateral, advertising efforts
- Brand ambassador activities to fly the flag for the company (i.e., sponsorship, field days, expos, etc.)

Section 3 – Account management activities

What do you need to put in place for your expectations of servicing your account base and how much time might this take? List in your plan:

- Account reviews to be done and when
- Territory time management plan
- Designing your account management review process
- New product solutions you will bundle and market to the existing client base

Section 4 – Sharpening the skills

What skill development are you going to commit to for the next year? The Trusted Advisor always believes in constant and never-ending improvement of skills such as:

- New referral language and process skills
- Developing a great sales process
- Creating more urgency around commitment from clients
- Time management training
- LinkedIn training
- Great questioning processes
- Presentation skills training
- Proposal writing
- Learning how to get the most out of the CRM system

Now you have a plan of attack, one where you can tweak as you go along and check in on the key measures of success and committing to the appropriate tactical responses to achieve it.

On the next page is a sample of the one-page plan, one that has the sections that worked for a client of mine, with all the numbers changed.

THE 90 DAY SALES PROFESSIONAL ONE PAGE SALES PLAN

KEY OUTCOME

Sales to increase by $ 200,000 from $ 500,000 to $ 700,000 for the financial year

KEY STRATEGIES

1. Increase intensity in new business prospecting
2. Calling on existing clients to create re-orders of consumables
3. Develop product knowledge in the new XYZ range
4. KPI / Accountability Scorecard

KEY TACTICS

Goal Area 1 - Increase intensity in new business prospecting

To do new business phone calls per week each Monday
To create linked in invitations in Linked In Premium
To ask for referrals from all clients over the last 3 months

90 Day Actions

1. 20 calls per week x 12 weeks
2. 20 linked in per week x 12 weeks
3. Create referral language for all sales calls

Goal Area 2 - Calling on existing clients to create re-orders of consumables

To set up meetings of all clients to talk about ongoing needs

To put together packages of good, better, best

To re-activate lapsed customer accounts for consumables

90 Day Actions

1. To hold 6 business meetings per week
2. To design an "upsell" package to increase AOV
3. To seek 1 opportunity per week for our Dept X

Goal Area 3 – Develop product knowledge in the XYZ range

To become the "go – to person" in our team for the XYZ range

90 Day Actions

1. Attend the NSW XYZ product training
2. Develop a page of FAQ's and answers for the team
3. To put together a sample kit for each sales person

Goal Area 4 - KPI / Accountability Scorecard

New Customers confirmed for 12 months – 100

Total Consumable sales for 12 months – 2200 units

Total sales for 12 months $ 700,000

90 Day Actions

1. 90 days sales turnover $ 100,000
2. New customers in next 90 days – 25
3. Total consumable units in 90 days – 560

Chapter 12
The Value Creator

The new buyer in this selling world wants someone who can tell them like it is; no BS, just the facts. They also want someone who they know might be a little more premium, but they deliver well and beyond what is expected.

Trusted Advisors know that it is gross margin that pays the bills and not the top line of sales.

This ability to hold margin is a skill any business owner will gladly pay a premium for in hiring salespeople in the new world of selling.

Protecting margin in the deal

Buyers will continue to ask us to justify our price. We therefore need to arm ourselves with some tactical ways of making our value argument. There will always be a lower cost producer in every market. It's a race to the bottom if you get sucked into that way of thinking.

When working with a client who has a premium product, I coach them on communicating to their buyers that in any market, there is *"always a low cost cheap competitor"* and I will deliberately accentuate the word *"cheap."*

When weighed against quality, *cheap* always sounds tacky. I have always thought that the customer doesn't always want cheap, but they do want value for money. The more we can focus on that, the less we have to compete with every *special* that hits the market.

Here are an assortment of tactical processes and arguments we can create in front of the buyer to ensure we capture every available dollar:

The apples versus apples comparison

There's nothing new here, but it is so fundamental.

The buyer will only disclose those things about the comparison offer to you which adds to their argument.

They will not disclose the things that will hinder it, so it's up to us to uncover the true facts. I have found that if we are positioning ourselves as being "best value not the cheapest," then we need to get onto the front foot and ask for more information about the quote that we are competing against.

Having coached salespeople in large agricultural capital purchases, we have found more often than not there is a difference in specifications, configuration, and inclusions that can be argued.

Do the work, ask for the evidence, and if you know the argument they are making is not factually correct, call them on it.

Assuming that the offer they have is *cheaper* at the front end, all is not lost.

When people say they can buy 10 to 20 percent cheaper, my standard line is, "There'll always be a cheaper alternative in any market, but if you give me the opportunity, I'll show you how we are the lowest <u>total cost</u> solution over the long term."

We are now putting a new definition of value into the buyer's mind. What I'm aiming to do here is to build an argument so when I get to the end and show it to the customer all written down, they can say, "You win in the long run."

Start to uncover all of the other conditions and variables in the purchase:

- Cost of consumables if it is equipment
- Specifications of the equipment
- Trade in value if it's motor vehicle
- Customisation if it's services
- Brand equity and testimonials if it is a service

Do they get all the features that you have in your product? Do they get the same back-up service?

How about account management?

Build a model of long-term value by asking how long they intend to keep the product and then divide any remaining differences over the number of years. Now you have the ability to talk in terms of any monthly or even weekly difference.

Mathematically, you should be able to beat "cheap" by offering a lower total cost solution. Hold your head high and say, "If you use my services or buy my product, in the long term, it will actually make you money."

Your value proposition

Buyers are interested in what you and your company stand for. It may not seem that way when you have an assertive buyer looking at you asking you to "sharpen the pencil" to get the deal.

In some ways, it is assumed that you have something similar to your competitor, at a price that is in the same ballpark. A value proposition is really a statement of your expertise and what that can do for your buyer to make your offer stand out.

I have always taught it to be encompassing these three elements:

1. Your target market – "We work with sales managers just like you."
2. Your results – "We increase sales by 32 percent and reduce costs by 25 percent."
3. Over a period – "Over three months period," or, "within 120 days."

A good value proposition doesn't sound canned, it doesn't sound prepared. It comes across as customised and conversational.

Understanding the negotiation game

The first book I ever read on negotiation was written by Herb Cohen, *You Can Negotiate Everything*.

Herb Cohen talks about "negotiation being the field of knowledge and endeavour that focuses on gaining the favour of people whom we want things."

I guess it was written at a different time when we were more combative in sales, where you either won or you lost. The book provided a number of techniques that you could use to get a better deal in purchasing just about anything in life.

I would recommend reading his assertive approach to negotiating; no one has all the answers.

Only a couple of years ago while at the National Speakers Convention (yes, they have a convention for speakers and keynote presenters; imagine the main conference room with all our egos), *I met Don Hutson.*

Don was the co-author with George Lucas of the book The One Minute Negotiator.

He had a different perspective on the subject and defines negotiation as "the ongoing process through which two or more parties, whose positions are not necessarily consistent, work in an effort to reach an agreement."

I think this definition of negotiation has always worked for me - a win-win approach that is mentioned in Don's book. Bottom line: negotiation should be fun as buyer and seller work from different positions to gain agreement, it's not personal.

I have found in working with salespeople that there are misconceptions of negotiation:

- The process has to be adversarial.
- There has to be a winner and a loser.
- You can burn your buyer during the process.
- It is a long drawn out process.

Trusted Advisors understand it is a part of selling and it can be a formal or informal process. A smart and experienced negotiator will know exactly when to bring you into a conversation and when to not. It starts with understanding there are three crucial variables which you want to be able to control as much as you can - **risk, alternatives, and time.**

Risk – The person who has the least to lose will negotiate hard. They are not on edge about the outcome and not tied to the transaction.

Number of alternatives – When there are plenty of vendors offering you what you need as a buyer, you are not locked into any alternative and can just search for the best deal.

Time – How about being pushed for time as a buyer or need to get the sale into your monthly sales figures as a salesperson?

Well-rehearsed experienced buyers know how to create a situation where they have you running around in circles. The question is, are you recognising the game and trying to short circuit it?

The nibble has been around forever in buying situations: the buyer simply bites off a little and then won't commit. They keep asking for more and more concessions.

How about the *gunslinger bravado* when the buyer looks like they just rode into town and bashed open the doors to the saloon? They can be heard to be saying, *"I can get a better deal elsewhere!"*

Fog is another technique, where the buyer shows plenty of interest and then deliberately gets lost in the background when the deal is about to be finalized. You can't get them back on the phone!

Splitting the difference has been around forever, where the buyer gets to a crucial point at the very end of the negotiation and then says to you, *"Come on, let's split the difference on this and get it done."*

The agent of limited authority is when the buyer will give the impression all the way through that they have the authority to do the deal only to find out at the last minute that they need to send it upstairs to get approval.

Ways to take back control

I have found over the years that there are a number of things you can do to short circuit the whole process:

Let the buyer win on the small points – Don't worry about winning on everything; let the buyer get some wins along the way. Save the big items for you.

Trade concessions – When you know what you have up your sleeve, you can better trade those points that you can give away.

Make each concession longer and a smaller amount – Make it known that they can't keep coming back to the well and wanting more.

"Compared to what" – When a gunslinger is claiming they can buy it cheaper elsewhere, ask them "compared to what?"

Always summarise the items before you give the final yes – Make sure that you have all items in front of you so they don't then come back and ask for more and more!

Selling in the New World Imperative:

To be a true value creator in the new selling world, you must be able to defend price at every turn and to build a rock solid case - this can only result in increasing conversion.

Chapter 13
The Deal Maker

Ultimately, in sales we need to write business. Trusted Advisors who can "walk their talk" and secure orders rather than just talking about them have never been more important in the new selling world.

The essence of deal-making is understanding people, understanding what makes them tick and the power of language. Salespeople need to be able to engage all stakeholders and then to earn the right to ask for the business.

Being a dealmaker means we need to start with the right mindset for success. Here are *seven short questions* to see where you think might be currently as a dealmaker:

1. Do you have a tailor-made sales process that you know, if followed with precision, can produce a predictable outcome?

2. Are you always learning new ways of presenting your message and choreographing your sales call?

3. Are you a student of buyer behaviour? Do you listen for words and phrases that the buyer continues to use or frequent questions that you are being asked?

4. Do you provide consistent customer experiences for your clients which makes it hard for anyone else to get close to them?

5. Do you study how to advance the sale? Do you know how to be assertive in a respectful way which doesn't break your trust?

6. Do you know your activity and conversion rates from incoming leads and also those that you self-generate?

7. Are you super-responsive and prepared to put in big hours when you know that the opportunity requires effort to wrap up the business?

The Mindset of the dealmaker

So, what are the things that dealmakers do that make them successful in gaining business?

1. Sell scarcity

Scarcity sells. It excites the brain. If people feel it's a scarce resource they go, "I'd better buy now!"

In business-to-business selling, having only a limited amount of product (or product that won't arrive from overseas for another two months), the idea of scarcity means, "if you don't get in now, I can't guarantee I can reserve it for you." There's subtle pressure in that.

2. Sell simplicity

Don't overcomplicate the deal. You can make a sale too complicated because you are trying to cover all bases in your communication. Instead of baffling buyers with offers, make your communication simple with language that involves a good deal of "yes" and "no problem."

3. Sell a bigger picture

Always look for the opportunities of getting a bigger sale by building a total solution. Look for the add-ons. How can your product be bundled or packaged with a service? If you've got a product, offer a service as well.

4. Sell an alternative choice

Don't offer yes/no alternatives; offer good-better-best, then use the "best" one to sell the "better". If you give buyers three options they'll choose "better" almost every time because the cheap one doesn't have the bells and whistles, while the premium one may be gold-plated and will blow the budget.

No one buys the lowest-priced wine in a restaurant because that makes them look like a cheapskate. But they don't buy the top one either. Your "better" can be 10 to 20 percent more premium than good, but your best can be priced anywhere you like. It's there primarily to sell the "better" one.

5. Sell the next action

Not everything can be "closed" in the first meeting,

especially in larger, more complex sales. Some people are quite nervous about popping the question, but as dealmakers, it's our business to ask how we can progress the business.

Give them a push, ask point blank, "Does this look okay with you? Can we do the paperwork?" If the buyer doesn't want to commit to the sale, then how about, "So what are the next steps from here?

Uncovering the four core drivers

The key to deal-making is to understand how buyers buy rather than just thinking about how you are going to sell to them.

The buyer wants to be valued as a person and they want their problem acknowledged. They also want to make sure that what you have to offer is going to be the right fit for them.

There are **four core drivers** of commercial business-to-business buyers, and mastering the signs of these will help you to create an automatic connection and rapport with your client:

1. *Make my life easier*

These people want it done for them. Price is not an issue. "Just make sure your product is easy to buy and easy to handle" is all these customers want.

They are just as likely to hand over a credit card and say "charge it" if they are convinced that you will take valuable hours away from them. Ask a behavioural style customer who knows what they want!

2. *Lower my costs or increase my profits*

How does your solution help them lower the cost to their organisation? Can you replace a fixed cost with a variable cost? Can you increase their sales and profits?

For example, a company's cost of a staff member might be $70,000 as a fixed cost. Your solution may only be an investment of only $30,000 as a one-off cost. It may take out the cost of a staff member. That's a pretty significant $40,000 gap in year one and $70,000 ongoing!

3. *Lower their risk*

Analytical buyers want their risks lowered. They will be attracted if you find a way that reduces a risk in going ahead. Social proof, testimonials, third-party endorsements, quality assured… these are all ways to lower risk. That includes investment risk (spending too much), fit the purpose risk (is this product going to do the job for me?), and kick-risk (will I get an okay from my boss for buying your product?).

4. *Increase our competitive advantage*

These buyers want to know that using your product increases their advantage over their competitors. Your job is to identify this need and to show them that you're providing an increased competitive advantage.

Exclusivity is one way of doing this if you are able to. If you provide a service and the client is willing to sign off on a substantial order with you, can you offer them the first opportunity in the market ahead of their competitors?

Selling in the New World Imperative:

To succeed as a dealmaker in the 2020's and beyond, you will need to know the emotional connections we can create with the buyer by talking the language of the four core drivers.

Chapter 14
The Rain Maker

Rainmaking is the process of creating a lead from multiple streams of opportunities, to nurture that lead and convert the lead. Rainmaking takes patience.

In the new selling world, we need to learn to be more patient than ever. The buyer will buy at their pace and not ours, so learn the new rules. The Trusted Advisor who can really understand why there may be a delay in the purchasing decision and then nurture the sale for the future will win.

Let's face it, some people don't return calls. That's always been the case, but it's more so now. Many new salespeople find this really hard to understand and especially new business owners in service businesses.

Buyers call everyone else back - colleagues, marketing, meetings, they return everything else and put sales at the bottom of the list and that's where it stays.

We as salespeople have just got to get over that discouraging fact.

I think we as salespeople get what we deserve sometimes. We leave a message and then when the person rings back, we don't have a plan for the call but simply say, "I was just ringing to see how you were and to have a chat."

The cost per seat

There's a wise old business saying that "salespeople have a cost per seat," In other words, the cost of that seat is what they are paid plus the cost of a company car or allowance and all other "on" costs. To make things cost effective, the company needs to get a multiple of that cost per seat. In some businesses I have worked in, it has been as high as a six times value multiple. In other words, the sales budget for that salesperson is six times what their total earn is to fund the business.

Anyone who can generate clients outside what the company gives them is a valuable commodity. If you are the type of salesperson who can make rain, you can "write your own ticket," you are an autonomous revenue producer.

The reality is that any business thinks there needs to be a return on the investment they are making on that salesperson, and if for a moment they believe they can get a better return on that seat, they will look elsewhere.

The new world of selling will look closely at this, working

out whether the human capital they have is really providing the multiple they need.

If I say I want you to increase your sales, you would automatically think, "I've got to get more customers." I'm saying, not necessarily.

There are always *four ways to increase sales* in your sales budget:

1. Creating more customers from your traditional segment or niche.
2. Selling more to your existing customers by increasing spend per transaction and how often they purchase
3. Reactivating your lapsed customers
4. Creating new customers in a new market segment

This is fundamental but overlooked by most salespeople I coach. The great thing is that when you understand the dynamics of these four levers, you then start to create a game plan moving forward to achieve it.

In so many businesses, the lapsed customer is forgotten - the marketplace is constantly changing and so are your decision makers. People change, the competitors change, products and offerings change.

Going deeper with the customer is the lowest hanging fruit for you to achieve your numbers. If they like you, they may be happy to buy more. Perhaps they are looking for the opportunity to shorten the vendor list.

Perhaps you have dominated a vertical segment of the market and it's time to dip your toe into another market. Can you partner up with someone who already has a stronghold in that market?

Your Rainmaker mindset

There are certain things that great Rainmakers do consistently that get results:

Being sticky in the market

Trusted Advisors are aware of opportunities. They look at competing brands and notice their logos and their ads. They are also aware of those companies who are using a competitor's product. Older salespeople in the trucking industry were good at this, scribbling down the name of the company whose logo is emblazoned on their competitor's truck while out driving on the freeway.

This enables them to approach those companies and say, "You're not buying our product, why not?" They're aware, they're on the lookout for opportunities, and they are "sticky."

Multiple streams of opportunities

Rainmakers are good at creating multiple streams of opportunities. When fronting the client there is not just one single stream of opportunity, there could be multiple. There are many roles one can play to get creative and generate opportunities. Networker? Prospector? Canvasser? Social media person?

These are many ways of making rain. It all depends on your buffet of rainmaking methods, your style, and your preference.

Big pipeline, big mojo

People who haven't got much in their pipeline are coming from the law of scarcity, so they hang on desperately to every name. A full pipeline creates confidence. Experience creates confidence as well. A word of warning: your pipeline is seldom as good as it looks. De-clutter it. The best do it all the time.

If you want to stop wasting time, don't have a whole list of people who are never going to buy - remove the rubbish. Constantly ring and check where they're at. Pop the entry on to a nurture list as soon as they're shaping up into a no.

Hunting while delivering

If you are a service provider, one of your biggest challenges is to keep filling the pipeline while busy servicing current accounts. Problem: there's no time for selling when you're servicing. Solution: you've got to find a way of hunting while delivering. You can do that by finding slices of time to achieve that. One way is to shorten your workday by just one hour. Create a slice of business generation amongst the busy implementation time. Spend an hour ringing your customers and prospects in the pipeline.

Time kills the deal

Each day that goes by means the opportunity becomes less and less possible in selling. Every passing day means time kills the deal.

The US sales trainer Brian Tracy called this the law of diminishing returns. Someone who is interested now will be less interested in three days' time.

Don't oversell

One trouble with rainmaking is the risk of overselling when trying to get the initial appointment. Some people give it all away at the start. When making appointments, don't try to convince the buyer upfront.

The aim of the call is simply to create rapport. So many salespeople try to get into a conversation all about what they are currently using and the virtues of your product; it's not the time for that yet. That's all. So don't oversell.

Be a scrapper

A "scrapper" is an American sales expression that means getting busy, getting off your backside, seeing people, ringing people, getting out there, and doing it. In other words, making sure that you're always able to get yourself back in that zone of making something out of nothing.

Great salespeople who are Trusted Advisors understand that when the chips are down, they need to perform. When the market is buoyant and buyers are buying, the job of closing out sales opportunities is so much easier.

When the market is tough, this is the time for scrapping. Creating a single focus on gaining opportunities, grabbing some smaller orders to get back into the game, networking with successful people.

BRAD TONINI

Chapter 15
The Trust Maker

The Trusted Advisor in the new selling world is committed to creating and building on this trust they develop with the client, not just because it is a perfect congruence with how they view the world, but also because it just makes sense in lowering the cost of acquisition and servicing of business.

A true Trust Maker understands the value of the client interaction and they respect their buyer's time. They will confirm in advance, will be punctual, and will work within agreed time frames for the meetings. They know that when they say they will do something that they are on show and better meet the promise made.

Being consistent with the client interaction, providing clarity in the way they explain the solution and the answers to client questions, and exhibiting competency provides a thought leader positioning in the mind of the buyer.

DWYSYW

Do what you say you will.

Every time I write this up on the board in the workshop I see faces nod in agreement. This is core to what buyers want, but then again, isn't it core to what we all want as human beings?

Salespeople have a history of making broken promises, so we deserve to be seen in a questioning light.

If you ask commercial buyers, a number will tell you that the salesperson was really helpful, they got back to them quickly, and were keen for the business, and then… nothing.

This is where so many people in sales get it wrong. Perhaps it's a short-term mindset?

Maybe it's all to do with not making a commitment to the industry they are in and seeing this as a lifetime commitment of business building?

Doing what you say you will, beyond the quote and the confirmed order, leads to a customer who is happy. That customer then in turn is happy to give you a testimonial and referrals.

Be one of the top ten percent who actually do ring the customer after the order has been fulfilled and ask if they are happy with the service they have received - it's a simple game changer.

Selling is a relationship business - it takes time to develop your client base and yet only moments to lose a client if you don't follow through on a promise made. Trust is earned and not given; it's all about being buyer centric and putting yourself in their shoes.

We often talk about the emotion attached to buying a solution. Sure, there is some logic in how buyers make decisions, but if we didn't believe that the salesperson plays a role in the relationship with the buyer, then all purchases would simply be made in the shopping cart.

Just like the relationships you have with your friends, they take time and they need constant work and nurturing to let the person know you care.

I think there is a trust test in sales. They may buy from you once, but will they buy from you twice?

The Triple A formula

Buyers are looking for three things in this new world in order for them to grant us permission to trust us.

The first A stands for *Agility* – they want it fast and they want you to be ultra-responsive. Gone are the days of saying, "I was out of the office all day at meetings." Find a way to get back to them!

The second A stands for *Acuity* – our ability to be proactive, to be curious, to be unambiguous, and to be generous. Can you read the mood and know when they are not happy and then repair the relationship?

The third A stands for *Accountability* – to be totally responsible for our actions and to stand by our word. To let them know if the shipment is running late or to provide a helping ear when the help desk is overloaded.

Trust is your competitive advantage

"<u>All</u> business is based on trust" is a saying you've probably often heard. It's critical in business-to-business selling. Business people talk to their colleagues throughout their working day.

Rapport is a personal connection you make with the buyer. It builds the relationship, leads to a higher sales conversion rate and more referrals. A common purpose and background builds trust. These are all part of a connecting point.

David Horsager, a friend and Hall of Fame speaker in the USA, wrote a wonderful book on trust: *The Trust Edge.*

David defines trust as "a confident belief in a person, a product or an organisation."

He has identified eight pillars of trust that were found to be present in all good teams, which he coins the 8 C's of trust:

Clarity *– People trust the clear and mistrust the ambiguous.*

Compassion *– People put faith in those who care beyond* themselves.

Character *– People notice those who do what's right over* *what's easy.*

Competency – *Confidence in those who stay fresh, relevant, and capable.*

Commitment – *People believe in those who stand through adversity.*

Connection – *People want to follow, buy from, and be around friends.*

Contribution – *People immediately respond to results.*

Consistency – *People love to see the little things done consistently.*

David's work is world's best practice and he is a leader in the field.

Think about it for a moment. How many of these C's of Trust are present in your organisation?

When you marry this thinking with the valued-based approach I talked about earlier, you have a new contemporary and relevant approach to selling.

Part 5

COLLABORATION IS THE NEW SELLING

Cold calling is dead, there is a better way.

Chapter 16
Connecting then nurturing the sale

Collaboration is the smart way to build business in the new world. It's low cost, highly targeted, and it gets a much better conversion rate… so that means good business.

In making a commitment to collaboration, we need to understand the value of investing in the sale by nurturing the sale; a hard sell approach simply won't work in the new world.

It doesn't mean that we don't ask for the business; of course, that's what we are paid to do. But, we must earn the right to ask for the business.

Ever been approached to be a connection on LinkedIn only to find that the moment you say "yes" to connect, you then receive the auto-responder with a long-winded spiel about what they do and how they can help you to gain more clients, save money on their finance, etc?

This hard sell approach is playing the numbers game and they have a mindset that *if I ask enough people, they will fluke a few sales along the way.* Trusted Advisors in the new selling world take a different approach to selling.

Connecting then nurturing

There is an etiquette with the new connecting world, have you noticed it? There are plenty who don't understand it and who will give you their life story straight after you have connected with them rather than working on a longer term strategy.

Are you in Sales Navigator in LinkedIn? It really is a must if you want to be current in the new market. I mean, what's the point in connecting with people who aren't your target buyer?

To be able to create lists of good quality leads to review is part of how we start the connection to the bigger future relationship. The navigator product allows you to be very specific - down to the postcode and to the level of decision maker and the roles they play.

Nurturing in the new world means you are willing to invest in a relationship, to create a dialogue without an agenda immediately, and to build for the long term.

Create nurture sequences

Business-to-business selling in the new world is about keeping proactively ahead of our buyer by building an ideal nurture sequence. This sequence can be developed in advance of the connection and might go something like this: first contact, second contact, third contact, then game day.

Call me old fashioned, but a great example of an offline nurture sequence, in terms of business-to-business, is a handwritten *thank you card.* It works well after the appointment to say, "Thanks for your time."

It's personal and goes to the core of being a Trusted Advisor. I love the handwritten thank you card with words like, *"Great to meet you today, looking forward to our conversation next Wednesday. Thank you."*

I guess some would say to just send them an email - it's the modern day equivalent. Nope, nothing really replaces the tactile nature of the card and the extra effort you have gone to in the mind of the prospect or client.

Another way of nurturing the relationship is to *leave something* behind, something to remind them that you were here. I leave a copy of my book. It means that when I've left the building, something remains to arouse further curiosity and hopefully prompt them to continue the relationship. It could also be a printed magalogue or an article of interest, collateral about the solutions you offer, etc.

A nurture sequence asks the question, "What would need to happen from the first contact sequentially to create a confirmed sale in terms of some logical next steps?"

Here are some examples:

The 48-hour phone call follow up.

Find a reason for getting back on the phone with that

prospect within 48 hours of your first meeting. Call and say, *"We were discussing opportunities…"* or, *"We'll make another meeting time for next week…"* or, *"Remember I said I'd get back to you about this?"* It's a reason, but be sure it's a "natural" one.

Send them an article, newsletter, or a blog.

It backs up the credibility of your last meeting. You might send something pertinent to what you were discussing. A short 20-word email is the cover note to which you can add a 2,000-word Word document.

Don't worry if they choose not to read your enclosure; the fact you bothered to send it is another small reminder that you're around.

Send birthday cards, anniversary cards, and Happy New Year cards.

This is a Joe Girard idea. Joe was in the Guinness Book of Records as the best salesperson ever.

Joe sold over 13,000 cars at retail for a Chevrolet dealership in the USA and was a guru of selling prior to the days of computers and databases. He wrote all of his own cards by hand.

Invite them to something.

Can you run a seminar? How about taking a table at someone else's event or perhaps a hospitality box at the cricket?

Invite them for a product demonstration.

Are you in the capital equipment or motor vehicle industry?

Is there an opportunity to have a demonstration of the product and get them to experience it?

The provocative social media post

Nurturing means keeping yourself visible in front of the client and prospect.

Think about how you can make your posts on LinkedIn stand out so that your connection world can stand up and take notice. It all starts with the headline.

There is a big difference between:

"How to improve referrals in your business" and *"7 ways to create more referrals than you could ever dream of"*

Working the negative angle would also have great payoff and cut through the clutter.

Something such as:

"Unless you implement these 7 keys to referrals, you risk not being in business next year"

Provocative opinions couched in postings with examples and stories will add weight to the argument and also adds colour to the post.

We need to get people to engage with our content at an emotional level and not just at a logical level.

Create your own podcast

There has never been a better time in history to create your own podcast or show to keep yourself visible. Again, this is a real solution to keeping your name in front of people and also for the Trusted Advisor positioning we talked about previously.

If you are in the business of selling services, this really is a must in the new world. Setting up your own podcast either as a recorded show or as a live show on Facebook or LinkedIn or YouTube has become very straightforward to put together.

Accountants, legal practitioners, consultants, and experts need to be seen, and other service providers can make sure they are always visible; interview people who can share ideas with your community.

What a great way to get closer to your clients than to spend 45 minutes on an interview with your client and having them reinforce to your audience how valuable you have been to their organisation.

Pre-record the show and then release the interviews on a drip feed basis to your email distribution list. Cut and paste the interview into a series of small tips that you can release weekly to customers. There are so many ways to take a body of work and use it for marketing and collaborating.

Some quick things to think about for a great podcast are:

- Create great original content – think about what you believe about a subject. It's only an opinion, but back it up so it makes a compelling argument.
- Interview people of interest – other thought leaders

that can provide a complementary topic to your area of expertise.

- Create a title for the podcast which reflects your brand, and if you are the product in your own consultancy, consider including your name. For example, New Selling by Trusted Advisor Selling is a series I created last year.

- Give the audience the opportunity to be a part of it by asking questions and giving feedback in the chat box, so you can answer their queries "live on air."

- Make sure you invest in good audio with an external microphone and not the one in the computer. If it's to be a video program on Zoom make sure you invest a couple of hundred bucks on getting some lights.

- Consider transcribing interviews with a program such as Rev.com, and now you have the basis of a new product such as an e-book.

Endorsements and testimonials

Our end game with collaboration is to become really good at asking for referrals, building alliances and communities, and other low cost business generation. Our first step to get into the rhythm of asking for referrals is to start by asking for testimonials and endorsements.

I have always found the law of reciprocity works well here. *"I will endorse you if you endorse me,"* especially on LinkedIn. Be generous and go through the database, and think of what you believe your contacts are good at; they will appreciate it.

With LinkedIn being so popular in making new business connections, it makes a lot of sense to build up your endorsements for skills that you have and also testimonials from raving fans.

New connections go there to have a look at your profile and the things you have done. But they will also notice what people write about you.

I can't think of anyone who wasn't happy to provide me with a testimonial as a client. The common response I get to a request for a testimonial or endorsement in writing is, *"Would it be okay for you to put something together for me?"*

This suits me as it provides me with an opportunity to write something that is going to work hand in hand with my branding and core messaging. Very infrequently will the client then make any changes to what you have suggested.

Of course, testimonials don't need to always be on LinkedIn and can be something that a client is happy to give to you over an email. Start gathering them.

Not only are they helpful in building a list of happy clients that you can show your prospective client, but this is also a critical step in climbing the ladder to what we will talk about next: gaining referrals.

133

Chapter 17
A mountain of referrals

The cost of acquisition of a new client will continue to rise as we march through the 2020's as traditional sales teams will simply make more and more calls and expend more energy and manpower to get a desired result.

The smart Trusted Advisors will make a commitment to creating new relationships by referrals and trusted introductions. This will not be a "nice to have." It will be the primary way to create new business success.

There are a ton of benefits to making referrals a priority in your business:

- Referrals cost you nothing.
- A quality lead is so much easier to convert.
- Referrals have a shorter sales cycle and a quicker sale.
- Referrals then create more referrals as you can remind the client how you first met and this then

creates a leapfrogging to the next one.

- It takes the pressure off price and being caught up in the commodity trap.

Why don't we ask for them?

We don't like to ask for referrals for a number of reasons.

We don't want to appear pushy.

My good friend, The Referral Coach Bill Cates taught me to make sure at the end of my correspondence I add the words, "P.S. Don't keep me a secret." What a simple, yet effective idea.

You wouldn't believe the number of times that a client says to me, "Are you taking on clients?" The answer is pretty simple: *"I am always in the business for more business."* A simple alternative could also be something like, *"We'd love to be of service to your friends."*

We have never been shown how.

The reality is that we have never been shown how to ask for referrals and so the process seems daunting. Many salespeople I have coached over the years also have never made a real commitment to getting them, hence it gets put on the backburner.

The problem is that if we don't go to work on a nice delivery, it will come across clunky and awkward.

We are worried about damaging the client relationship.

We're afraid our clients might see us in a lesser light if we ask for referrals; I don't think this is true.

We also have to get over the idea that we are being an imposition to our clients. The truth is that if you are doing a consistently good job for your clients, they will be happy to look out for you.

Don't want to be rejected.

Rejection is a necessary part of sales. Sales would be easy for everyone if we just simply converted 100 percent of our leads. The truth is that the average salesperson will get refused the business at least 66 percent of the time and for some, a much higher percentage.

What's the worst thing that will happen? So you get the occasional "no" or "not sure." It won't kill you.

It will cheapen my self-image.

Perhaps think about it all this way. Maybe your customer will see you as being a professional salesperson who is looking to be even more successful in your industry?

It's all in the way you ask really and when to ask. The language of referrals can flow off the tongue when the feeling is right and the customer is a raving fan.

No commitment to asking for them.

This is the big one for experienced salespeople. They know they should do it, they know the benefits of doing it, and they pick up most of their business that way. The only thing is that they are leaving big money on the table by not making it a habit and part of their sales process.

A mindset shift

Start with re-wiring your mindset with how you feel about asking for referrals.

Here are three great reasons why you should make a commitment to creating a process for asking for referrals that fits your style:

First, if you already have a trusting relationship with your valued customer, then they want to help you and you want to help them. Make it reciprocal so you are helping each other.

Second, you are in fact saving the person who has been referred to you time. Time is money in business and by you being referred to one of their friends or business associates, you are helping them to find a new vendor and not having to go to market.

Third, it makes the referrer look good. Plenty of behavioural style customers love to be able to say to their friends that *"they know someone who…"*

It feeds their ego.

Earning the right

Now that you have had my arguments for getting on the referral train, it's time to start building the process to create a magnetic system for attracting them into your business.

The truth is that we don't get referrals unless we earn them. Sure, people can give us names and numbers that don't amount to anything, but I am talking about the quality referral that converts!

Trusted Advisors in the new world understand that referrals will come in spades if we create a great experience with the client. Consider these questions:

Do you do great work?

Not just good work, I mean the type of work you do for a client that makes them go WOW. Would they rave about you to others? Do you constantly exceed expectations and go the extra mile?

Are you responsive?

I mean really responsive, the sort of responsive where you are returning the call within minutes and they are again saying WOW.

Do you give more than they expect to get?

Do you surprise them by adding something into the solution they were not expecting? Do you deliver ahead of the project end date? Does the order get shipped a day early?

The foundations to getting referrals

Be generous

Start with asking them if they would like more business.

Let them know that this is how you get your business and you would be happy to keep an eye out for them.

I had a freight salesperson come and see me many years ago when I was in the diary business to pitch for the business. He opened the conversation asking me who an ideal client was for me and then proceeded to tell me that he had over 200 clients in his portfolio who might be a good match.

The law of reciprocity

Get referrals from people in exchange for referring them. This is a reciprocal arrangement. The legendary motivational speaker Zig Ziglar was known to say, "Help enough people to get what they want and they will in return help you to get what you want."

There's no right time.

People often say you have to get referrals at the end of the sales call, "after we have done the business." That's nonsense. You can ask for referrals at the 10-minute mark, halfway through, or at the end of the sales call if the feeling is right. Bill Cates, whom I mentioned earlier, says, "Whenever value has been given and recognised."

Thank the referrer.

We need to say "thanks," but a lot of people don't. A phone call is best, an email is okay. Anything is better than not doing it. Respect the referrer and keep them informed; they will then give you more.

Keep reminding them.

Just because you have asked once and received a referral doesn't mean they won't give you another one. It's okay to go back to the well and let them know that you are always in the business for more business.

Over the years I have had customers give me three to four over a three-month period and a dozen or more over a lifetime.

The language of the referral

It's really all about how you ask for the referral to be good at gaining referrals.

One way of approaching the referral is to not see it always as a serious pitch you are making. Learn to be cheeky and casual with your approach.

Letting your client know that you *"always have room for more clients in your business"* will remind them that you have a commitment to building more business.

Try saying something like:

"All of my business comes from word of mouth and I would love to be of service to your family, friends, and business colleagues."

Another approach that I have seen work well in selling situations is when you create a conversation that is all based on a win-win relationship:

"I wanted to have a conversation with you about how we might be able to both help to build each other's business in a reciprocal arrangement."

Think in terms of simple language that you feel okay with using on an ongoing basis. Try and experiment, but make a commitment to asking.

Selling in the New World Imperative:

Referrals are the lifeblood for the Trusted Advisor. Not only do they create a higher level of conversion, they also cut down your selling time to help you build a business.

Chapter 18
The trusted introduction

The top rung on the ladder for great salespeople is a trusted introduction, either face-to-face or via the email handshake. This is the best you can get in the spirit of collaboration.

I was doing some coaching work with a company in Geelong many years ago, and I had developed a really healthy relationship with a team of six people selling in the printing industry. Over a conversation, we had chatted about the relationship they had with the Geelong Chamber of Commerce, a really influential body for business in Greater Geelong.

The sales manager mentioned to me that their business had been a gold sponsor for the Chamber, which was a substantial investment and an important relationship for the Chamber.

I wanted to do business with the Chamber as I knew they were looking at ways to bring more value to the members, and their members were a great fit for my business as they had salespeople and locally did not receive quality sales training.

My thinking was to run a series of sales breakfasts and members would attend, enjoy the experience, and then we could have a quality conversation about how I might be able to help their team. I asked the sales manager if he could introduce me to the CEO, to which the sales manager replied, "We can do better than that!"

He then picked up the phone and rang the CEO (they were always going to take the call given the business they were doing with the Chamber) and he introduced me to them on the phone right there. He said I was doing some great work with the team and that I could add massive value to the local members.

The CEO invited me around for a coffee immediately and the sales manager even drove me there to meet her. After a brief 20-minute conversation, the deal was done for a monthly sales breakfast for members for the following six months.

That's the power of an introduction from a trusted source.

When someone has an existing relationship, the trust is then transferred to you by way of introduction. The person then feels almost compelled to meet you as they don't want to let the person who introduced you down.

The secret is to be as specific as possible. I didn't say to the sales manager, "*Can you introduce me to anyone you know?*" I was specific about wanting to get in front of the CEO of the Chamber.

This is really where we are playing the quality game and not the quantity approach. Quality introductions will reduce your time in building your business, and in the new world, if you get good at it, the sky is the limit.

Be specific

The secret to gaining well - researched, quality introductions is to define exactly who would be a great customer for you.

Most people cast the net too wide and then have that embarrassing situation where the person they have referred to you is just not a great buyer for you. Define your ideal client right down to the bootstraps, nominate industries, and the role in the organisation you need to have a conversation with.

Profile the size of client you like to have, the number of employees or the dollar turnover. Do you want only companies that have multiple offices and are nationally based due to the scale of your offering?

Take the time to explain it; the customer can't help you when you merely say, "I would love some introductions."

An email handshake

The trusted introduction can also be all done via an email handshake. Just ask your client if they wouldn't mind introducing you by simply sending the contact an email and copying you into it.

This is a soft approach as it's not done over the phone, and it could be a great way to step into this powerful way to collaborate. The process is then very simple. As soon as you see the email arrive at your inbox, make a note to initially jump in on the email conversation and introduce yourself if they don't return the email promptly.

As a matter of habit, I give the person a couple of hours to reply, and if they don't, I am on the email with some suggested times to line up a face-to-face meeting on the back of that initial contact.

It's powerful, as I have found that the person who has been referred is almost obligated to meet you out of respect for the person who referred you.

Selling in the New World Imperative: The conversion rates you can achieve from trusted introductions are well over 50 percent, and if they are in the market for what you have to offer right then, close to 100 percent.

Chapter 19
Building networks and strategic alliances

Collaboration selling requires us to think different from the average salesperson. One way of being a great collaborator is being good at building great communities who have the same interests as you and who hang out in the same places.

It could be a local networking group, a referral group where there is an organised way to cross-refer clients and prospects to each other, a breakfast community like my Friday School of Sales in Melbourne, or the professional association of which you may be a member.

The power of networks

As salespeople, we need networks.

It's amazing how people want to help you in business if they like you and you respect the relationship. Never forget the source of the invitation to a network, and lay praise on them for being the conduit.

Think of your own industry group: the alumni from the university you went to, especially if they have a business group. How about the opportunities afforded by judging awards or being involved in the executive team meetings in running the network?

Be the person on the front door handing out the nametags, a sure fire way to get to know everyone. Look for those who are attending for the first time and make them feel comfortable. They may just be the next referral source for you.

During the COVID-19 pandemic, I interviewed Wendi Dawson from The Melbourne Business Network for her thoughts on the future of networking in the new selling world.

She explained to me that while the MBN was principally a network based on live events where members exchanged cards, ideas, and referrals, they had to pivot to be relevant by offering a series of networking events online.

We chatted about the fact that moving into the 2020's, there would be a place for both live and online events in the future as people had gotten used to this form of meet up and it was time efficient.

My dad always talked about how business works: "It's not what you know, it's who you know." This became his mantra as he developed relationships in business, a key part of the success for a man who left school in year nine.

When you have something in common, like a common

meeting reason, it means that you can develop instant rapport at the function and then segue into a conversation as to when would it be an appropriate time to meet up.

So, what networks do you need to get involved with right now?

Creating your own community

There has never been a better time to create a community of like-minded professionals.

LinkedIn allows you to form your own communities through their groups function. Start a group and invite your connections to join you. Then you can control the communication to the group as the owner.

You can post your ideas and invite others to post their ideas, and then get the community talking around a provocative subject. Now you have engagement from the group.

The benefits are endless. You are now the Trusted Advisor, directing the traffic and providing an expert opinion to the group. The community is formed and you now have a vehicle by which others are drawn to you, and the community can become a fertile ground for relationship building and collaboration.

Communities don't need to be set up in LinkedIn necessarily. There are plenty of available membership sites like Kajabi that allow you to form a membership community and then post questions of the community and have them reply.

My point is this: when you develop your own community of raving fans, you are able to collaborate with them and cross-introduce them to valued associates of yours. You become the source by which other people meet and there is real value in that.

Strategic alliances

Trusted Advisors in this new market ask themselves - who else sells to the same market as we do and would they be someone who might be up for a conversation about working together?

Where would it make sense for us to partner? How would we present a united front, a total solution to market so there was an ease to doing business?

It might involve bundling of a solution, perhaps something innovative. Is there something in your range that might be a strategic advantage for another company to have it as a part of their range?

I know of a client who sells software, but they don't have the infrastructure to also sell the hardware to their clients. It's not their area of specialty, and for them to get good at it, they would have to invest a good deal of time and money.

So why not find someone who has the specialty in that area?

They consistently do joint presentations to provide a total solution to the market and it automatically creates a perception in the mind of the buyer that they are a bigger enterprise.

Service providers have been doing this for years. My solicitor many years ago was part of an allied professionals group where they had a solicitor, accountant, bookkeeper, and financial planner all in the same building but all running individual businesses.

They actively promoted each other's businesses by having fliers and business cards in the reception area, had a joint letterhead branding they all used. They also regularly had functions together where they all introduced five or so of their clients and in a boardroom-style event with a guest speaker.

Think of the benefit for the customer: no running around, no need to source new providers. So where is the opportunity for you right now? Who provides a product or service where it would make sense to build an alliance for cross-referring?

Road test it and make sure they deliver on their promise with one opportunity first. Then check in with the client you have referred to see that they did a great job.

Think "one to many" conversations

The opportunity to talk to a group of interested parties, say 20 to 30 at a time, provides a unique opportunity for them to sample what you do. It is also efficient; it is a better use of our time to talk with a number of potentials by being the guest presenter and sharing some ideas rather than trying to introduce yourself individually.

The business of speaking automatically positions you as a thought leader and as an authority people will want to seek out for an opinion. When you speak well and provoke thinking and questions flow, then you have engagement.

Look for groups that make sense such as an industry group, franchise meeting, local business networking forum, or on a bigger scale like a national conference. There is always a need for speakers as delegates need value.

The Executive Connection (TEC) and the CEO Institute are examples of groups that bring together CEOs on a monthly basis where they have guest speakers come and talk about a topic of interest.

Develop a talk, and as you gain confidence, look for ways of making it as entertaining as possible with a clear call to action at the end.

New business acquisition is all about collaborating.

Part 6

PROACTIVE ACCOUNT MANAGEMENT IS A PRIORITY

Virtual and "live" account management is here to stay.

Chapter 20
Sell more by strategic organic growth

I ask a good deal of sales managers on my journey where they think the company will create most of the "strategic gap" between the current level of sales and the desired level of sales, say 12 months from here.

The answer is "organic growth." The only problem is that I get the feeling that this is more of a hope than really any planning. I like the idea of proactive planned organic growth, the sort of growth you have when you meticulously put strategies and tactics in place to achieve the growth.

In 1987, I attended a presentation by Murray Raphel from the USA at the Pan Pacific Direct Marketing Symposium in Sydney. Murray presented a paper to the attendees that was so simple and yet so powerful. The sales formula he outlined was the original, and many have since claimed it as being theirs. Sales = number of clients x frequency of purchase x average order value.

To repeat:

    (1)   Increased number of clients

    (2)   Multiplied by frequency

    (3)   Multiplied by average spend

In his presentation, he put up on the flipchart a simple 10% increase in each of these variables, and hey presto the sales overall didn't just go up by 30 percent but 33 percent. Try it.

The compounding effect really starts to get interesting when you start to multiply out numbers into the thousands of customers and average order values into the hundreds.

At the time of the conference, I was in the diary business and had a problem. Almost all customers only bought once per year and usually bought the same diary systems each year.

So, over coffee, I sat there and contemplated, "How do we get them coming back this year, not for just one diary purchase but maybe get them to buy something else too?"

A new range of promotional products was born: things like coasters, t-shirts and caps, in an effort to get clients to buy a wider range and more often. We already had relationships with our clients. They liked what we did for them, so why not?

Over the next two years, we were able to convert over 25 percent of our top 250 client base into a client who also bought promotional products, pens, and other merchandise. What we actually found was that many of them were already buying these products elsewhere, so they were receptive to it.

If you look at companies today like Kogan, really that's the business they are in. The IP is in the CRM and ordering system through compelling offers and not necessarily the product itself; they can get any product from anywhere.

This is the lowest hanging fruit we all have in our own selling business, and yet we don't spend enough time on it. In the new selling world, this is the first priority and the most strategic way to increase business.

Grab a piece of paper and start to work on it.

To increase the <u>number of clients</u> you are focusing on:

* Incoming leads

* Conversion rate

* Sales process

* Speed of response

* Strategic alliances

To increase the <u>frequency of purchase</u>, you need to brainstorm:

* Other complementary products that go with your offering

* Increasing servicing or call cycles

* Creating an automated billing cycle (i.e., Stan or Netflix)

To increase the <u>average order value</u>, you will need to:

* Create good, better and best options on the current offering

* Create a bundle that makes sense (for us, it was a diary with gold blocking of their name in gold leaf)

* Use the language and process of upselling the sale

I remember when the accounting software providers all changed their models from clients buying the software to an automated subscription based model many years ago; it was a total game changer in the industry.

It was all about how we create an ongoing income stream by locking in the frequency of purchase - very clever.

The ascension ladder

One way to create planned organic growth is about how you can provide an aspirational model to clients, so they can go deeper in the relationship with you and to embrace a bigger offering.

Many years ago I was introduced to some different thinking that I hadn't considered through the *Dan Kennedy* direct marketing world.

Dan Kennedy was a pioneer in the direct marketing copywriting business. He is the guru in the USA. He wrote direct marketing sales letters for his clients and charged them anywhere from $10,000 to $20,000, and this was many years ago. He coined the phrase "The ascension ladder."

Simply, an ascension ladder works on the idea that your clients come into your world purchasing at a certain level. It might be at the very bottom of your ladder of offerings to sample the product and service you have.

Over time, once they get accustomed to the level of service and quality of the products you have, they want to purchase more and to upgrade from the entry level of product they have purchased from you.

If you plan an ascension ladder, you will have the next three or more rungs of your ladder pre-planned and then offer periodically an opportunity to upgrade for only a little bit more, either by email communication for smaller sales or by sales presentation if you call on clients.

Clients aspire to climb the rungs of the ladder. Just look at the frequent flyer status credit model from the airlines! I know some executives who will take a return trip from LA to Melbourne to rack up some last minute credits so they don't lose their status at the end of the year.

What are the upgrade options for your products and services? How can you plan the multi-stepped sales process for your clients so they are aware of the different levels available?

Can you create a club or an inner circle membership that clients may aspire to be in?

Chapter 21
The account management plan

We have already talked about the fact that one of the keys of being the Trusted Advisor is to look first and foremost to our existing relationships for the organic growth we need in our business. The development of an account management plan just makes great business sense to make sure we are planning multiple moves ahead in developing each relationship.

Salespeople ask, 'How can I get more clients, more clients, more clients, more clients?' We are always looking for the next opportunity, the next hunt of the next piece of business. Why not go deeper with existing customers? It's easier.

There are lost sales everywhere in business-to-business selling. Plugging holes in this bucket is a great place to start to ensure that we are building off a solid foundation.

Here's a checklist:

- Where are you not being responsive in dealing with current enquiries?

- How about not converting the prospect into a buyer because you haven't wrapped a compelling proposition around your price in terms of price justification?
- Where do you need to sharpen the saw in sales skills?
- Where can you look for up-sells, on-sells, and cross-sells rather than just letting the customer go?
- How about more product knowledge to sell more?

The Account Management Plan

A detailed account management plan for your existing top 20% of accounts makes good business sense, but it's amazing how infrequently this is done in my experience. Consider these thought starters as a part of the development your plan:

Account CRM details

Have you got all the details correct? All key influencers, job titles, and notes up to date of all previous meetings? Get the data right to start!

Current buying patterns

So what has each account purchased? Is there a trend in terms of seasonality to the business? Do they usually take the "special offer" or are they happy to buy all the "bells and whistles?"

Opportunities that exist in the account

What opportunities currently exist, what aren't they buying

right now? Why? Are they purchasing part of the range from another vendor?

Targeted slow release of new products

When I consult to sales teams who sell into retail, it is important to release the products in the range to keep the interest of the buyer. Don't overwhelm them but give them an opportunity to absorb. Have you ever found yourself hearing the buyer saying to you, "I didn't know you did that"? Buyers need to be repeatedly shown new products in different ways.

Quarter-by-quarter planned promotional activities

So what promotional activities do you have planned for the top 20 percent of the account base? Are there targeted promotions that provide an incentive to purchase more?

The Ferris Wheel

I mentioned Joe Girard earlier, the Guinness Book of Records best salesperson ever. I love one of the concepts he talks about in his book, *You Can Sell Anything: the Ferris Wheel Concept.* He explains that all customers purchase from us on a cycle and go around and around just like a Ferris wheel turns. As the Ferris wheel goes around it then comes around again when it's the right time to buy again.

If we look at a car dealership, we can see that on the journey to a repeat purchase, the customer would have multiple purchases from us through parts and service before they come around to buy again. Networking like crazy with service and parts would therefore make sense for us for the next sale!

So, what does your Ferris wheel look like? How long does it take for your customer to come around to buy again? Is it 12 months, three years, or, as in capital equipment and other larger purchases, five to seven years?

Map out the lifecycle of purchase in your industry and work out where the critical points are on the journey to repeat purchase. Make a commitment to database the journey in your CRM system and then create alerts to remind you of when you need to reach out to them.

Does anyone else need to be involved? Does anyone else have contact with the customer in the meantime to provide them with consumables or other add-ons?

*Selling in the New World Imperative:
Great account planning just makes
good sense in developing a bulletproof
exterior to the client relationship. Once
you have an account management
process, you can then develop the best
way to serve the customer via the
blended account conversation which
leads to the next sale.*

Chapter 22
The "virtual" account review process

The new world has taught us that for some clients, it's much more efficient and effective to do servicing of their account via Zoom or other technologies. We can do back-to-back account servicing calls without having to leave our desk and to manage the "long tail" of small account renewals without having to go on the road and meet face-to-face.

Every business has a long tail - those customers who need to be serviced but who spend very little in your business. By getting smart on how we service the long tail, the cost of retention of some business could actually drop in the 2020's if you follow the virtual servicing model, and then going to work on acquiring new relationships.

The new challenge is for salespeople to master the virtual tools, be succinct in their communication, and engage our customers without being in front of them.

The "virtual" account servicing model

Working your way through your database and looking at the best way to serve your client is smart business. Where there may still be an opportunity for organic growth and spin off referrals, then get the face-to-face visit.

Most of the other business can be serviced via Zoom and other technology - and here is the kicker, the client may even prefer it! Truth is they may not see the need to see you either.

So how do we transition some of the long tail in the business over to the virtual world?

Our goal is to sell the idea to clients so they can see the value of the virtual meeting, setting up a frame of reference of what the agenda and purpose of the meeting is, and getting engagement of the client while on the call.

So what makes a great virtual account process?

- *Create* – send to your client in advance the things you would like to cover and get feedback on.
  Create some importance around it. Key discussion points and outcomes.
- *Connect* – ask how they are, find out where the company is at. What's the biggest challenge they are facing?
- *Clarify* – make the purpose of the meeting clear at the beginning of the call, a time frame established.
- *Context* – agenda, key discussion points, and things they would like to walk away with.

- *Content* – questions for the buyer to consider, things you want to ask during the meeting.
- *Commit* – your agreed action plan and statement of next steps you can email to the client.

If you consider what time it used to take you to drive out to the customer's premises, go through the items of business, and then make your way back to the office, you are way ahead in terms of how you manage your time!

If you prepare how you will get the customer engaged in the process virtually, then you have maximum effectiveness at the same time. Create a virtual meeting process and then craft it to find the ideal way to create engagement and how a 30-minute call can be used to maximum effect.

Zoom has become the generic

I wish I had shares in Zoom or Microsoft for their Teams product, as they have become the hot thing in business. Now a clear picture of the person is right there in front of us and all of their office is on display to us.

Good video and audio can be enhanced by a microphone for about a $100 investment or a video camera if you want TV quality.

Take a tutorial in Zoom; there are plenty of them. If you are stuck, help is only a click away. Go on to Upwork and post a project for a Zoom-experienced professional and there will be no shortage of people who will be able to help you from all corners of the globe.

Get familiar with the product. Practice and record yourself and play it back to see what the customer will see. If part of your week will be working from home, consider how you will set up a studio or a "set" in your home office where there is a well-arranged plant, print, and vase, etc., to fill the frame.

Making impact and buyer engagement

Now is the opportunity to add value and create differentiation in the market by thinking how to make this medium effective and not just efficient. It's easy to fall into the familiarity trap, when rapport has been established and not their Trusted Advisor.

Engagement can come from sharing your screen, having them load up their notes, spreadsheet, or PowerPoint, and now they are playing the role of presenter.

Some things to consider as you now look into your home office in terms of professionalism and engagement are:

- Your *"set"* – The appearance when someone jumps on to a call with you. The professionalism of a carefully placed print, the bookcase, or the virtual background.

Lights are cheap, and you can set up a little area of your home office with a couple of lights on stands for under $300.

They are worth it.

- Your *dress* – You are still running a business meeting, be careful. You don't need to be in full business dress, but if you are normally dressed in a suit with an open shirt and pocket handkerchief, perhaps consider the sports jacket? At a minimum, grab the business shirt.

- *Your angle of the camera* – Have you noticed how many people when interviewed on TV shows have the computer camera looking up at them when they are talking? Now we are distracted with the ceiling behind them, the nose hairs popping out and other stuff. Remember to check behind you. Not great having that wedding picture from 1995 in the background with your blonde mullet that was fashionable all those years ago.

- *Your agenda* – What are you planning on covering? Can you pop your main talking points on a card and tack to the side of the computer so you can maintain eye contact?

- *Your support materials* – Do you have the facts and figures all loaded up so when you share your screen it's all there ready to go rather than fumbling around to find it all? Spreadsheets, PowerPoints, order reports, delivery reports, etc.

- *Your shared screen experience* – Will you share your screen with others on the call? I would recommend having the desktop of your computer as blank as possible and also having your PowerPoint or spreadsheets loaded up and ready.

Selling in the New World Imperative:

The number of salespeople working from home in the new world has changed the norm for the way we service our existing accounts. Create a process that works, and not only will you be able to save time and money, you will also create more time for the hunting of new accounts.

Part 7

CUSTOMER EXPERIENCES, NOT JUST SALES CALLS

Your buyer is asking, "Do I really need to see you?"

Chapter 23
No more winging it!

The days of being unprepared or "winging" the sales appointment are well and truly over.

The future of selling is all about putting a premium on the face-to-face sales appointment, so don't stuff it up! Buyers have got used to not meeting up in recent times and this places the onus back on us to provide a good reason.

The habitual sales call on a regular cycle is being questioned as we sell relevance in a new market. So the sales call now needs to continue to grow into a customer experience, a moment of truth where we need to wow and create memorability.

Our job as Trusted Advisors is to be strategic, to think multiple moves ahead and know what outcomes we are driving on each appointment.

Creating a great context by framing up the meeting when you begin as well as delivering relevant and timely content will be a finely tuned balance in making the customer experience come to life. Our buyers are asking themselves:

Is this salesperson really here to help me or are they just trying to get the business?

Will this salesperson be here for the long haul?

The Five P's of the customer sales experience

The Trusted Advisor who truly gets it will be taking the buyer on a journey, to challenge their thinking and to provide alternatives the buyer hasn't even considered.

They will also be memorable and be able to mount a compelling argument and do it in a respectful manner, always acknowledging the position of the customer.

There are **five P's** of the customer sales experience to make each meeting a winner:

Prepared

Ready to share the purpose of the meeting, to prepare in advance of the meeting, to truly understand what's in it for the customer to be listening to you.

Purposeful

Being clear on what you are there to say – not just turning up because you always have.

What do you want the buyer to think at the end of the meeting?

How about what you want them to do?

Proud

You will always be attractive to the customer when you show your pride in the company you represent. Talk about your "why" you turn up to work each day, how you help other valued customers.

Present

Are you truly present at the meeting? Are you able to listen and repeat exactly what the customer wants and needs? Can you tell stories of other valued customer experiences?

Process

As a Trusted Advisor, these are the minimum expectations for the new rules of engagement:

- Research always done in advance of the sales presentation
- Respectful of the buyer's time and with an agenda
- A stepped game day sales process to follow but delivered in a conversational way
- A segue into something new that the buyer either hasn't seen before or re-packaging of an existing idea
- Tailoring of questions at critical moments to create the theatre in the sale
- Use of relevant and current visual aids to keep the attention of the customer
- A clear summary at the end of the visit where the actions steps are clearly spelt out

- The ability to hold attention and create an impression with storytelling and analogies

Make it a moment in time

Salespeople can easily come across to the buyer that they are in a hurry to get to the next sale. Being present with the buyer is all about putting other distractions to the side.

If the customer is coming to you, make them feel welcome and not just by giving them a cup of tea or coffee, I mean really welcome. Remember their kids' ages, where they live, what place they were going to travel to. Remember something they didn't expect you to remember.

Prepare in advance of every meeting. Not a long preparation, just 10 minutes will do it in some cases.

Review their previous orders, look up any quotes that didn't convert, check with customer service to see if there have been any issues with returned goods or unfulfilled promises.

How about accounts? Are they all paid up? Has collecting money been a challenge at all?

Now review your notes on file and re-acquaint yourself with what you know about the customer, the person behind the transaction and not just your next car payment.

Selling the context as well as the content

I interviewed on my weekly NewSelling podcast program a

good friend of mine from the USA, Lou Heckler. Lou is a world-class speaking coach who helps experienced speakers become even better.

When I interviewed Lou on the program, he said something quite profound about the speaking experience which I think has a direct application to the selling experience face-to-face.

He mentioned that every speaking experience is all about the context and the content of the speech, and he is right. Same with selling.

Ask yourself what it would take to make sure that your selling message is relatable and will improve the client condition and add value?

Not just simple features and benefits statements, really powerful emotional connections.

The context is how your solution will fit into their plans, how it will save them money, or add to their sales results.

The customers mind is processing what you are proposing and putting the idea into a context, like a sorting process.

Is this a better offer than what I currently have from the incumbent?

Can I sell this concept upstairs given that we have a number of other priorities right now?

Create your game day process

The secret to an experience is to create a sales process which reflects your style and personality but also makes sense by being flexible.

I have seen many sales processes over the years, some as long as 12 to 15 steps, which is complicated by any stretch. Our objective must be that we can recite the steps in our sleep, but not to send the prospect to sleep!

The danger here is making it so rote learned that the buyer doesn't feel very special; a great sales process really makes the person feel that the questions you are asking them are off the cuff and based on great listening and intuition.

It's Game Day, and it's up to you to choreograph the sales call the way you want it to go. I call this the theatre of the sale.

Like the director of a stage production, our job as Trusted Advisors is to read the sales situation we are in and try to move the conversation to the crescendo we are looking for.

I call this flow the rhythm of the sale.

There will be times when the sales call is running with great energy, feeding from excitement about their business, your product, or perhaps a discussion about someone you both know.

There are also times when the energy flags and the buyer is weighing up the information you are sharing or the questions you are asking. By being totally focused on the buyer, we are watching for this.

We are reading the look in their eyes, their keenness to check out information we are presenting, their body language, their level of distraction with incoming calls or emails blinking up on the screen. These little things all matter.

One intelligent question

Research the person and research the company beforehand so you already have something under your belt when you turn up. *One intelligent question* is part of the rapport-building process.

I mention in the theatre of the sale chapter that I have a favourite way to start most meetings.

My favourite approach is, "I couldn't help but notice when I was on your website a few nights ago that your business - *(insert here something you found out)*."

The most important words in that line are *I couldn't help but notice when I was on your website*. You can really customise however you like after that.

With that sort of opening, two things will happen. First, they will be impressed that you spent your time out of hours preparing for the sales meeting, and second, they will ask you what you thought of their website!

What a contrast! Most salespeople turn up uninformed and blurt out something like, *"Hey, what keeps you awake at night?"* And the buyer goes, "Really? I had a guy come in this morning from a rival company. He'd been on my website, he googled me and asked me some pretty interesting questions. Do you know anything about me?"

Strategic questioning

Build more questions behind that one based on the feedback they give you. Try to uncover their level of authority and how decisions are made, what outcomes they are looking for, and if they can afford it.

Are they happy to share who they currently use for the product or service you are looking to supply? Any issues with the current vendor?

How about timing to accomplish the project or when they have the capital expenditure for the larger scale solution you are offering?

Let the buyer tell you their story, if they are comfortable to share. You will also be able to get a firm idea of their style bias as they elaborate on things of interest to them.

Make empathetic statements back to them as they are telling you their story. Our goal here is that we want the buyer thinking during this part of the process, "This guy gets me."

Don't underestimate the teasing out of an answer, the verbal cues of *"tell me more about that,"* or the non-verbal nodding as they expand on a point and your making of notes as they elaborate.

Segue then demonstrate expertise

After I've asked questions and developed a deeper understanding of their current state, this is the time when an attuned buyer will normally ask, *"Tell me about your product and tell me what you guys do."*

By the way, if they are not on the front foot and asking you that question, you can simply ask that question of yourself. Segue with something like:

"Well, I guess I should tell you a little about our company", or, "May I ask, do you know much about our business… XYZ Company?"

Now is the opportunity to make sure you have the demonstration phase of the presentation all rehearsed, yet looking conversational and spontaneous. This is the bit you should know in your sleep.

Move into your message to market that drives your competitive advantage (see chapter on developing your message to market) and make sure you cover three key areas of uniqueness in your offering.

Demonstrating your expertise means also being strong in backing up the points you are making with evidence of guarantees about your products and services.

Evidence is a critical part of the journey as a Trusted Advisor. Consider the following:

- Printed collateral you can leave behind
- Your website on a tablet you can easily access
- A demonstration of how the process/system works
- A process visual that explains important differences in the market

- Testimonials and endorsements from happy clients

Punctuate your demonstration by asking all the way through how the buyer feels about what you are showing them.

Testing the water

We need to constantly test the water with the buyer.

Testing the water is an opportunity to see if the two of you are on the same page. You don't have to wait until the end of the sales call to ask if we can proceed. Good Trusted Advisors will be suggesting we move forward throughout the meeting.

You might just say, "Sales of this product are at a premium, do you want me to check on stock now?" You can use any of this language during the sales process if you feel you're enjoying great rapport and you want to move the sale along:

- *"If you were to go ahead, which option do you think you would like?"*
- *"Let's have a look through the proposal that's in front of you. Are we on the right track?"*
- *"How is the solution sounding to you?'"*
- *"Let's assume I could create an option that allows you to cash-flow the project over (period of time), would that be attractive to you?"*
- *"This model looks like the best fit. Do you want to see if we have it in stock for delivery next week?"*
- *"Why don't we start with a trial order now to make sure you're happy with the product or service?"*

- *"Based on what we've talked about today, how do you want to progress with this?"*

Confirming the business

There are no shortage of books that you can download with all the "closing approaches" from over the years. I am not sure we need 37 different closes but just some ways to respectfully ask for the business. Here are a few targeted approaches that have worked for me and are even more relevant for the new world in which we now sell:

1: Recommendation. A Trusted Advisor is an insider, a type of "business friend." Knowing the buyer's needs and the capabilities of the product on offer positions the salesperson to make an informed recommendation. This requires sincerity.

Use language such as:

"Based on what you have told me, my recommendation would be…"

2: Good/Better/Best. My dad always taught me to provide the buyer with three ways to say yes and not just a yes/no response. By providing three options, we now have assumed they will buy, it's just a matter of which one is the best fit for their needs.

Price your solution *(good)* and then allow for a *better* option at about 15 to 20 percent premium. The *best* option can be as much as 50 percent above the better as it is there to make the *better* look amazing.

3: Social proof close/similar situation. Offer a similar situation. Talk about someone else who bought it. Say, "I had another customer who was considering these options. This is what they decided to go ahead with. It seems like a good idea for you too."

If they need more convincing and want to get on side with stakeholders, you can go one step further. Give the phone number of the person you're telling them about and add, "Give them a call." Multi-meeting sales requires the buyer to know what is next. Don't leave it all open ended. Next steps is the key, "where to go from here," and give them an idea as to where you want to take the conversation.

This is how we confirm the business in the new world.

Selling in The New World Imperative:

There is no shortcut to success in the new selling world—do the work and don't wing it! Create a sincere and tactical approach as buyer time will be at a premium.

Chapter 24
The great theatre of the sale

In the world of customer experiences and not just sales calls, the Trusted Advisor in selling is a master of the theatre of the sale in bringing the presentation to life.

Not from the point of view that what we do is to put on a performance and that there is nothing true and real about our selling, only in reference to how we need to make an impression in front of the buyer and be memorable.

If people do buy on emotion and justify their purchase with logic (not new but a goodie), then we need to be experts in creating an experience that engenders an emotion. The buyer won't necessarily remember every fact or recommendation we are making, but they will remember how we made them feel when we leave.

It's a matter of noticing and being aware when you have created a golden moment and then advancing the conversation to create action.

Like true theatre, ask yourself how you are going to "stage the experience," the timing of the meeting, and the pace that goes with it.

What do you need to prepare in advance?

Is your messaging congruent? Are you providing evidence and mounting a business case like a true Trusted Advisor?

Regular role playing in teams, mastering the art of storytelling, and analogies are all in your toolbox for the theatre of the sale and are the "must have" skills for the successful new salesperson.

Are you visiting them at their office or are they coming to you where you have the opportunity to control the variables controlling the stage setting as you like?

Theatre is differentiation and leaves the conversation being memorable. This might include the use of props like a Montblanc pen to position you or a car parked out in front of reception that has received a fresh wash, vacuum, and polish. Don't underestimate a look of success.

If you are calling on a regular customer, my feeling is that they shouldn't be exempt from the experience. It's easy to fall into a false sense of security that this account will never leave us. Perhaps one way to look at it is to imagine the regular call is a new call. How would you now prepare?

One of my best attended breakfasts I run for members of my Trusted Advisor Selling Institute is the "Theatre of the Sale." I think it's popular because it's a theme that's been lost to the next generation of salespeople as they're so consumed with online selling.

When we spend the time together in the workshop discussing the theatre of the sale, I cover up to 25 different ways of creating great theatre to master the customer experience. Here are a few of them:

1. Telling stories

Stories build social credibility. Stories are visual. They create a sense of authenticity. Storytelling is a big part of the theatre of the sale. Stories enable buyers to put themselves in the picture. Many conferences have replaced 90-minute keynote speakers with 15-minute talks which are mostly story. Use storytelling as a core part of selling. The idea is to tell a story and make one memorable point that sticks.

The format for sales stories wraps itself around one character. Another client you've been working with is ideal. From this character, there's a simple three-step format: (1) the problem, (2) your expertise, and (3) problem solved.

Example: *A client of mine called David had a similar problem and was thinking about the decision you're making right now. He called me because I'd helped him before. I came in, we had a chat about it, and decided to do this-and-this and guess what? He had a most successful result.*

It's a "similar-situation" story. That's all it is.

You should rehearse your storytelling and get the stories

down pat. It doesn't matter if you are telling the same stories over and over again; it's the only way to get really good at telling them. Remember the customer is hearing this story for the first and perhaps only time.

Make your stories team stories. Brainstorm together as a team and then discuss the stories that you can all borrow for when you are in front of a buyer. Make sure the stories are real and be respectful to not share any confidences about the client.

Once you get used to telling stories in sales, you then look for the nuances that make a story come to a life. It may be the way that you place emphasis on a word, a phrase, or how you look at the buyer at a certain time in the presentation.

2. The magic of sound bites

Politicians use memorable sound bites instead of making complex policy statements. A "sound bite" is a one-liner, a four-to-eight-word catch phrase. They have learned the power of slogans that stick in the memory.

Some sound bites might seem silly, but recent US and Australian elections prove that they stick in people's minds.

Remember "Stop the boats," or "Make America great again" They cut through!

In a sales situation, you could use expressions like, "family values," "30 years of market leadership," "partnering for long term." These all work well as they position your business in a matter of a few words. Create your own sound bite out of a message that you think will resonate with the market. Don't be shy about repeating it often.

3. Proposal Foreplay

I had a meeting with an insurance salesperson some years ago. We went through a discovery process to find out what I wanted to insure and he came back to me a week later with the proposal. "I've got it here…" he said. He kept touching his proposal and kept talking.

I was sitting there thinking, *Give me the damn proposal!*

The insurance salesperson continued, "You said that you were looking for around about $X savings in terms of your policies. In here," he tapped the pages, "I've put together two to three alternatives for you between $800 and $1,400."

I'm sitting there thinking, *give me the proposal I'm ready to go!*

What was he doing?

He was doing what I call "proposal foreplay." He was building up what was inside the proposal knowing that as soon as he handed it over, I'd stop listening to him and go straight to the price. He needed to build value first.

While the salesperson held that proposal in his hand, I was totally engaged. As soon as the proposal is handed over, he loses power and my attention. The same thing applies to handouts in courses. As soon as I give out a handout, the attendees start reading it and I lose their attention.

4. Benefits before features

Salespeople are trained to talk about the features of their product. I believe the better way is to give the benefit first. Suppose you're selling a recording device. Tell them what's good about it: "One of the great things about these devices is its portability…" However, salespeople tend to start with the specifications, which is less interesting. Talk the benefit first and then move into the features.

Like this (when selling tractors): "Our business is about saving on fuel and maintenance costs…" instead of, "This new tractor a horsepower range from 140-400…" The benefit statement came first, the feature came second.

Go back to where I talked about the four core drivers of commercial buyers and think about how you can lead with one of the drivers such as "make your life easier" and then tie to it a feature of the product or service.

5. A picture tells a thousand words

If we were to monitor how much talking we do during the sales appointment, we might be amazed how much we talk compared to how much the buyer talks.

A way of building a compelling argument with fewer words is to present to our buyer a visual that can be unveiled or a model you have developed which really shows one of your competitive advantages in an instant. It may be picture of the three circles of advantage you bring to the market.

Think in terms of a demonstration, a process visual, or a short video you can show on your tablet when you are discussing ideas with your buyer.

BRAD TONINI

Chapter 25
The great language of the sale

Selling is all about language.

The more sophisticated the question, the better the chance the buyer will see you in the light of a true Trusted Advisor.

Develop a broader vocab and you will be well positioned to be able to hold your own in a management team or board conversation.

Notice what words get attention, which ones complement your approach, and the words your buyer uses when you are in a conversation with them. In its basic form, there are just some words that have always worked and will always work.

Here are some words that I recommend you work into your sales presentation:

- Easy
- Guarantee
- Results
- Save

- Fast
- Latest

These words are clear, focused, and visual. Some people favour the word "free." It's a hot word, there's no doubt about that, but I am always working with salespeople on value adding and not discounting.

Bunnings – The coal face of selling

My wife works for a charity and she asked me to help out with cooking sausages at the local Bunnings to help raise funds. Goodness knows I have bought enough of those Bunnings sausages over the years, I thought it's probably about time to help out.

I was on cooking duties, which means cooking about 400 sausages for the morning (which is a smaller mid-week number) while my wife and my eldest son Josh served the local tradies. While grilling another tray of sausages, I listened to Josh's routine as they bought their sausage with tomato sauce and onions. Buyer behaviour is interesting.

You might be interested that about 90 percent take up the onions option but the soft drink option may only get about a 5 percent response. I suggested that he might like to change his approach.

I suggested he should ask, "Would you like a drink with your sausage?" I guess it seemed like a logical approach, and let's face it, it has been so successful for McDonalds with their, "Do you want fries with that?"

The response doubled.

Then, when he became more confident, he said, "How about a soft drink with your sausage? And the response rate went up to about 20 percent overall.

That's the power of suggestion, or, as we say in Trusted Advisor Selling, the power of the Recommendation Close.

A change of a word, a phrase, a pause, or change in tonality can all create a different outcome.

Words that sell, words that don't sell

Remove the words that don't sell and replace them with words that create a connection to the buyer. Some customers are visual people. They might say, "I see this for my company in the future."

A more auditory buyer will say something more like, "It sounds like…" and then the kinaesthetic buyer who is more of the heart style will be talking about how "it impacts upon the team or the culture of the organisation."

Any advantage in the new world is an advantage. Listen out for the words, the phrases, and the types of questions your buyers use and you will learn a great deal about what is important to them and how they buy.

Change your vocab by creating new substitute words that will create more impact. For example, change:

- Price to *investment.*
- Quote becomes *proposal.*
- Product range is *total offering.*
- Payment terms are *payment options.*
- Deal is *agreement.*
- Customers are *partners.*

Great rapport - builder language

Questions create a sense of genuine interest in the other party. They warm up conversations and the answers provide helpful information in your quest to fulfil customer needs.

When you are 100 percent present with the client, one question just leads to the next one. Get immersed in the client's condition and what they are trying to achieve and the time will fly in the appointment.

Here are some questions that work well for me:

- "Can you tell me more about…?"
- "Can you give me an example of where that was a problem for you?"
- "Am I right in saying…?"
- "If we could do this, would we be on the same page in terms of expectations?"
- "What's your thinking about the time frame for implementing the project?"
- "What's the potential upside of this project after completion?"

- "Are you a one-page proposal person or a 30-page proposal person?"

- "If we were to provide a competitive bid to you, would we be a candidate for your business?" (That's a beautiful question because it's hard to say no.)

Price and negotiation frames

As a Trusted Advisor, one of our core skills must be to hold as much margin in the confirmed sale as possible.

We talked about this in the value creator section previously covered.

The skill of being able to couch a price objection, to build a business case, and to ultimately make an authoritative comment is a valuable skill.

Here are some <u>negotiation frames</u> I have used for many years that have really helped me:

1: "Is it okay if we just put money aside for the moment?"

In other words, we don't want a conversation about the money for the moment. Let me try and provide a little more value in the options first.

2: "How much too high is it?"

You are trying to get the buyer to speak with much more clarity, in exact terms.

3: "How far apart are we?"

Is it 10 percent, is it 20 percent? It's time to be specific so I can see if we can be of assistance to you.

4: "I'm not saying I can (cover a spread in the price), but if I could, can we confirm the business?"

In other words, I need to get the buyer's permission to go ahead and try to find that gap.

5: "Do you have a budget in mind?"

Fifty percent of your buyers will never give you a budget. That's okay. The other 50 percent will. That's pretty handy information, isn't it? What have you got to lose?

6: "What would you like me to leave out of the proposal?"

If someone says to me, "You're 20 percent dearer than your opposition," I want to make sure the buyer knows that you can't have it all, so let's collaboratively take something out of the proposal.

7: "In the three-part solution I have outlined, which solution do you think is right for you?"

The buyer says, "I want that one," and I now know which one the buyer wants. It's about working the conversation around to that admission.

8: "If money wasn't an issue, which solution sounds right to you?"

The buyer will say, "I like that one," then we respond with, "Okay, now we have to find a way for you to afford it."

9: "How about if we were to…"

In other words, "If I were able to get that price, that product, that bundle, would you buy?" I'm getting the buyer to come along with me.

Chapter 26
Your message of uniqueness

Knowing your competitive advantage, even if it's a slight advantage in a competitive market, will give you a way to mount an argument in the new world.

Salespeople who do not have a clear message of competitive uniqueness and how they are different from their competitors will not succeed in the new decade.

At the core of Trusted Advisor Selling and creating real value is an understanding of how you are different from anyone else in the market.

The buyer has a decision to make: stay with the incumbent, a low-risk decision where they get what they know, or take a chance and go out on a limb with this new entity and to give them a chance.

Most conservative buyers will stay with the former unless there is a real reason to change, such as a mistake or series of mistakes by the incumbent or perhaps a price advantage.

In a bid situation where you are asked to pitch for the new business, either one-to-one or one-to-many in a board or management team opportunity, your ability to come up with a succinct rationale for using your business is critically important.

The message of uniqueness is a must-have in selling today. It reminds the buyer that yours is a professional outfit and there's a consistency across the whole sales team. It also reminds the customer why they shouldn't entertain a lowball offer.

When I ask participants to answer in the class in a coherent way, "Why should I buy from you?" there is rarely a coherent and well-thought through response. There are sound bites given and throw away phrases but nothing usually that flows professionally.

Why have one?

So, why have a prepared message of uniqueness you can recite and deliver to any existing or new client in the market?

1: To increase the professionalism of your selling process.

To position you as a true Trusted Advisor. You look like you are aware of where you have a real edge.

2: *To create a consistency* across the sales team or enterprise.

There is nothing more impressive when a sales team can individually recite their message of uniqueness to customers across the counter or on a business-to-business sales call. Great way to engender a team sales culture as well.

3: To hold margin in the sale.

The marketplace is as competitive as ever, and the buyer knows which buttons to press to get what they want. Your message to market creates a compelling reason why your company or brand and your reputation are strong enough to command a premium price in the market.

4: To remind good customers why they shouldn't consider a "lowball offer."

By introducing your message of uniqueness into your buyer conversations or account reviews, it puts doubt in the mind of the buyer when entertaining moves from a competitor.

5: To increase your self-esteem and confidence in the negotiation process.

A good deal of sales success in the top 10 percent of salespeople comes from keeping a fragile confidence in check and self-doubt under control. By repeating the message of uniqueness on every sales call, it really sells you on why you do what you do and will bullet-proof your mojo.

Building your message of uniqueness

Now it's time for a well-rehearsed, yet seemingly "just thought of it" message to market. A one-line statement and a longer explanation about what makes you different.

1: Umbrella Statement

A one-line statement, a sound bite that you can use anywhere in a meeting that makes you and your solution unique.

So if I was to be delivering my own message to a sales director or small business owner, it might sound something like this:

"I work with salespeople, sales managers, and business owners to increase conversion of leads by implementation of my Trusted Advisor selling method."

2: Three main pillars of uniqueness

Now create a brainstorm of ideas as to what you think makes your business and your offering unique. Don't worry if not everything is absolutely unique; it's the combination which makes it unique.

Examples might be:

A more comprehensive product range, quality products and services, family-owned business, our account management structure, or perhaps the strength of brand.

Again, if I am presenting mine, it might look like this:

"I am a solo practitioner who customises all of my work and is a sounding board to your sales team."

3: Evidence and self-evident statements

Now back it up with evidence: this could include things like demonstrations, testimonials, or endorsements.

An example of saying "our extensive product range" might be, "We have over 210 models available in our range so we can provide one that fits your needs."

The real value of a great message to market is that we know it's a great qualifier also really. If you are giving your message of uniqueness to a potential buyer and they are not seeing value in what you are presenting to them about your point of difference, it will help to determine that you are not the right person for them, but equally they are not the ideal customer for you.

Delivery of the message

The last part of the theatre of the message of uniqueness is in the delivery of the message. You never want to appear that the answer is rehearsed and rote learned, even though in reality you have used the same message in every sales call.

The use of a pause, time to reflect while the question is being asked, adds to the theatre and the suspense of the answer. I always preface the answer with something like:

"If I had to think about it, a few things come to mind as to what separates us in the market…"

And then I start to articulate a few key things. You also don't have to "press play" when giving the answer. It doesn't need to be perfect.

Your buyer will be super impressed you know succinctly the answer to that question.

This is worth rehearsing and getting it right. Write your answers on a pad, flesh them out, and keep it with you when you hit the road for a sales meeting. If you are a part of a larger sales team, spend some time brainstorming and using the collective wisdom of the team.

We have preconceived ideas as to what the customer values and when you think about it, the person who should be centre stage is the customer, so ask them!

Reverse engineering

Many years ago, when I started in the sales consulting business, I was designing my own message. I had a number of things down ready to discuss with the customer and see how they would register with them.

I asked one of my clients if I could enlist their help. I told them at the time that I was designing a new website and wanted to get their feedback. I asked them why they used me in their business.

They replied to me, "I really enjoy all of your material and I know the team gets a lot of benefit from it, but what I value more than anything else is my ability to get your opinion on things. You are my Trusted Advisor! I guess a sort of sounding board before I go ahead with any important sales decisions."

Trusted Advisor Selling was born off the back of that one conversation.

Reverse engineer your message from your best raving fans.

Ask your customers why they use you and what they most value from your relationship with them.

Using your message of uniqueness

This process is not just for the face-to-face sales call where we are pitching our credibility to multiple decision makers around the boardroom table.

New business conversation

Your first appointment is a moment of truth. There is theatre in how you present your ideas and make your points. The message of uniqueness can be used in the rapport building segment or casually at the urn in making a cuppa with the buyer.

You can also segue into the message by making a more obvious frame up.

"Well, I guess I should tell you a little about our company and how we work with our clients."

Existing customer review

Whether that be on a regular 90-day cycle or an annual review of performance and reflection on previous business volume, the MOU can be used to reinforce your value to the buyer.

"As you know, our positioning has always been to…"

Meet and greet networking

Using a sound bite from your message of uniqueness to position yourself in 10 seconds is a key to creating a great first impression. At our Friday School of Sales, I ask everyone to introduce themselves in 10 seconds or less as good practice of being able to sell your message quickly to a group of strangers.

Written emails / confirmation emails

When you are reconfirming the points from your meeting or confirming discussions in a summary email, there is an opportunity to bring in a pillar or evidence statement into the email as an opportunity to restate your value.

*Selling in the New World Imperative:
Knowing your competitive uniqueness
is critical to the positioning and
marketing of your business. As a
Trusted Advisor, we can create a
stealth process through our messaging
face-to-face.*

Are you equipped to succeed in the new market?

Selling in the new world will never be the same as the old days.

Are you equipped with the tools you need for success? Are you committed to always be better than you ever were before?

Selling in the 2020's decade is more complex and not for the faint hearted. How invested are you in your self-improvement to make this a sharpened skill?

The transactional content has been taken away and put into website shopping carts, leaving only conversation and expertise for the salesperson to perfect, in which instance we are all Trusted Advisors.

You need to devise a strategy that works for you, one with a clear focus on results and outcomes and a plan to achieve them. However, I stress that a sale that is not good for the buyer in the long term is no good for the salesperson either, which means a Trusted Advisor salesperson must provide good value.

How do you provide value to the buyers? By helping them

make informed decisions, by sharing your expertise, by translating difficult product-speak into everyday language. That's why you're there.

Buyers can get the facts online, but they can't get guidance. And having looked after the buyer, how do you look after yourself by holding the margin on the deal? Answering these questions is what being a value creator is about.

A Trusted Advisor knows that being a great dealmaker is not just about serving the customer, turning up on time, and sending back a proposal; it's much more than that. Trusted Advisors are paid for results, good ones. Results that are so good that buyers keep coming back.

Trusted Advisor Selling is not about order taking, taking an incoming enquiry and converting it into a sale. It's about generating business, which I call "rainmaking." When you master this, there is no upper limit to your earning potential.

What a great honour it is to be an active member of this old noble profession, to be able to make a difference in other's lives, and to create clients for life.

Enjoy!

Brad

Additional resources and tools to help you convert more sales

Here's how to experience more of the Brad Tonini Trusted Advisor Selling Method:-

Website - www.bradtonini.com

The Monday Morning Mojo - our weekly video program

Weekly sales program – NewSelling

Join our LinkedIn Group – The Trusted Sales Advisor

Brad's Trusted Advisor Selling Institute runs:-

A monthly "Friday School of Sales" breakfast

A number of half and full day programs in the Trusted Advisor Selling Method

Virtual and face to face sales training for your sales team

The Sales Leaders Roundtable – an intensive group of sales managers and business owners mastermind program

www.ingramcontent.com/pod-product-compliance
Lightning Source LLC
Chambersburg PA
CBHW051051050726
47592CB00002B/474